Fries!

AN ILLUSTRATED GUIDE TO THE
WORLD'S FAVORITE FOOD

Blake Lingle

PHOTOGRAPHY BY JOE JASZEWSKI

PRINCETON ARCHITECTURAL PRESS
NEW YORK

Contents

I DON'T HAVE THAT ONE FRY MOMENT,

like my father and I cruising to the beach, sharing boardwalk fries, and then discovering pirate treasure upon burying our feet in the sand. Most of us don't have a single fry moment. We have *fry moments*.

Fries are everywhere, and as a child, I was equally concerned with devouring all fries and winning Nickelodeon's Super Toy Run. McDonald's was my obsession, not only because its fries were as close to edible perfection as my noggin could imagine but also because toys accompanied the fries.

Not much has changed since I became an adult. I've yet to meet a salad that dissuaded me from ordering fries with my

claim okra is best fried in California, but if the
ttempt to pilfer our corndog, that same
ill join you in arms—and then we'll quickly

food brands an indelible mark on our brains.
covet it, and we'll detour vacations and drain
ulge in the best, if only to taste whether the best
a childhood memory. It has even graced the
e our fine country's finest restaurants.[2]
fort foods are the star of the plate. Not fries.
adfastly and subserviently accompanied other
ut reservation or prejudice. They have
yers with jalapeño poppers, cheese sticks, and
ey are the proletariat of American foods.
are about to revolt. They're discontented with
h status. They're tired of carrying multibillion-
ations such as McDonald's on their back.[3]
t that despite being the most widely sold food-
in the United States,[4] they're considered an
They're ready to be the subject of a plate (and

WHAT IS A FRY?

nch is absent from this book's title, for three
as I'll discuss later, the French may not have
fry; two, in some of the earliest references to
s used more as a verb than as an adjective; and

meal. And while I don't in

days (not for reasons of n

those reasons do exist), I

Three times per week on

I cofounded and co-own, I

"Why fries?" was the

question when we started

this a bad time to start a l

always fail?" (Folks often

My answer, which was als

deserve their chance to be

Of course, that was a

response. Fries reached e

and have grown in prestig

decades. Nevertheless, at

more attention—and still

burgers, and steaks have

them to the same caste as

beans, and dinner rolls (at

One person's cast-off

however. Despite being th

are a ubiquitous type of co

group that is scientifically

blue.[1] That's partly becaus

I'd question your palate—

claimed my grandmother's

less than ambrosia. Comfo

unleashes patriotism. A S

kidney if yo

French ever

Southerner

win the war.

Comfor

We crave an

wallets to in

is better tha

menus of so

Most co

Fries have s

entrées with

shared the f

hot wings. T

But frie

their side-di

dollar corpo

They're ups

service item

afterthough

of this book

Note that fr

reasons: on

invented the

fries, french

three, call me superstitious, but I feel that pasting *french* to *fries* would surely cause this book to fail—and I would much prefer it to fail on the merits of my writing.

The definition of a classical fry is a potato cut into strips and deep-fried. Absent from this definition, yet implied, are the following modifiers: *unadulterated* for "potato" and *served hot* for the whole. The classical fry has five characteristics: unadulterated (not coated), made from potatoes, cut into strips, deep-fried, and served hot. In other words, breaded fries or potato chips would not be considered classical fries.

The contemporary fry challenges each of these characteristics:

- **Unadulterated.** Sodium acid pyrophosphate and beer regularly coat modern fries. Coatings help fries remain crispy and colorful.
- **Made from potatoes.** Sweet potatoes are common fries yet aren't even distantly related to the potato. The potato is from the Solanaceae family and has tomatoes, chili peppers, and even tobacco as cousins. Sweet potatoes are from the Convolvulaceae family. Coating allows most any vegetable—not to mention Coke or Twinkies—to be fashioned into a fry.
- **Cut into strips.** Circles, spirals, cubes, wedges, cylinders, and tick-tack-toes are common fry shapes these days (see Chapter Three). We're even working on a ring fry and a tube fry at BFC.
- **Deep-fried.** While most restaurant fries are deep-fried,

most household fries are baked. Fries can also be grilled, barbecued, and fire roasted. Some form of cooking is necessary; raw potatoes are toxic.

- **Served hot.** Snacks like Pik-Niks and Whatafries are served cold, in cans and bags, respectively. (The question of whether these are fries at all is the Chip Conundrum, which I'll discuss below.)

It's difficult to define the contemporary fry. Yet for the sake of this book, I'll provide a definition anyhow. The contemporary fry is "any vegetable, cut any way imaginable, coated with anything edible, cooked any way feasible, and consumed hot."

The above definition has two notable restrictions: *vegetable* and *hot.* I plan to stick to the botanical, not the culinary, definition of a vegetable. Thus, tomatoes, cucumbers, squash, zucchini, pumpkins, peppers, eggplant, tomatillos, chayote, okra, breadfruit, and avocados—all fruit—won't count. Nor will legumes (which are sort of fruit anyway) such as green beans and snow peas, seeds such as wheat and corn, or fungi such as mushrooms and truffles. This also eliminates fried butter. As for hot, while I enjoy Chester's Fries as much as the next intoxicated person, *Fries!*, much like fries themselves, needs a little structure. It also provides an answer to the Chip Conundrum.

Potato chips are fries' hate child: according to lore, disgruntled restaurateur George Crum invented potato chips in a fit of rage after a customer whined about his fries being too thick. However, in this restaurateur's opinion, those (hot) chips were, in fact, fries. Chips (the American, not the British, version, which are certainly fries) are fries if they are made of vegetables and served hot. Chips can be fries, in other words. When served cold, however, chips remain—and fries become—chips.*

Fries have evolved. The contemporary fry definition is valid only until we get to the last chapter of this book. Beyond that, only Demeter knows....Fries will evolve beyond the limits of *Fries!* And this fry cook is stoked to try them.

WHY FRIES MAKE YOU HAPPY: THE JUNK PHILOSOPHY AND REAL SCIENCE

Why do we make fries? Because they make us happy. Why do fries make us happy? Because they do. Science need not corroborate this claim. The simplest reason is often the best reason—just ask Occam and his razor. In the *Nicomachean Ethics*, Aristotle propagated the philosophy that happiness is the ultimate purpose of human existence, and thus, if

---

* This raises the Hash Brown Question. By the above definition, are hash browns fries? Like chips, hash browns, to most of us, are a distinct commodity. Unlike chips, hash browns are almost exclusively composed of potatoes and served hot, which fits our fry definition. So yes, hash browns are fries. Much like Tater Tots and BFC's own Po' Balls, hash browns are simply reconstituted potatoes. They're even called "home fries" occasionally.

THE FRY SHAKE

FIRST: Find two hands. Both of yours will suffice. But one of your own and another one of someone else's is better.

SECOND: Each hand should make a fist. Quickly note how it resembles a potato.

THIRD: Say "potato it," and then pound the fist potato into the other fist potato.

FOURTH: Explode both hands while frantically wiggling the fingers and say "french fries."

FIFTH: Smile at yourself or your partner and acknowledge a handshake well done.

1

2

3

4

13

something makes you happy while not being excessive or fleeting, it's worth pursuing. As long as you don't overindulge, fries can walk beside you on the path to happiness. I can assure you of that. I have thirty years of experience.

Junk philosophy aside, science does, kind of, corroborate the "fries make you happy" claim. Nostalgia is a powerful sentiment. A study conducted at the University of Illinois found that "comfort foods may be consumed to positively pique emotions, to relieve negative psychological effects, or to increase positive feelings."[6] To make you happy, in other words. Comfort food also evokes patriotism, which is linked to happiness.[7] Chinese philosopher Lin Yutang said it best: "What is patriotism but the love of the good things we ate in our childhood?"

Potatoes make you happy. A large chunk of the population suffers from sugar sensitivity, which can cause mood swings and depression. Dr. Kathleen DesMaisons, in her book *Potatoes Not Prozac*, calls potatoes "an antidepressant in a brown package," and she recommends taking a skin-on potato, or even skin-on oven fries, before night-night time (I have kids) to raise levels of serotonin, the monoamine neurotransmitter that promotes well-being and happiness.[8] Toss some salt (which lowers stress hormones and raises the hormone linked to love)[9] on those oven fries, and you'll be even happier.

HOW TO ENJOY THIS BOOK

I'm not a historian; I'm a fry cook. Before opening BFC, I knew little about fries other than my opinions. Thanks to my business partner (Riley Huddleston, current corporate executive chef and beverage director, LondonHouse Chicago) and some trial by fryer, I've learned more about fries than the baseball card mogul inside me ever imagined.

Research for *Fries!* was conducted between naps and after ingesting fries. The book is loaded with heaps of conjecture, food verbiage, exaggerated yet appropriate jokes at the expense of the French, and sarcasm.

Fries! describes how to make fries but does not provide explicit recipes. A few recipes have sprouted in Chapter Four, but this is not a cookbook. If you're looking for that, I'd recommend *French Fries* by Zac Williams or, if you can read French, *Le livre des frites* by Anne de La Forest.

Chapter One

THE ORIGINS OF FRIES

The truth is, we can only speculate on the wheres, whos, and hows of the origins of fries. But, like any good historian, I will not let scant evidence prevent me from making a foregone conclusion. Below, the origins of fries (within the context of the contemporary fry definition) are presented through the countries that, in my unprofessional opinion, possibly cooked the first fry. The challenge of this exercise is determining when a severed and domesticated vegetable first met fire. A tool, an edible vegetable, and a source of heat must've coexisted, in other words. Cutting tools may date back 2.6 million years,[1] and cooking may date back 1.9 million years,[2] yet edible vegetables may go back only 180,000 years.[3] The five-year-old in me appreciates that time line:

I started researching around 5000 BC. I didn't find anything until 2500 BC, however.

2500 BC: EGYPT

Humans are quick to fault God for pain and suffering in the world, but do these same humans credit God for the joy of fried food? It often relieves my suffering. One of the earliest references to frying[4] is in Leviticus 2:7: "If your grain offering is cooked in a pan, it is to be made of the finest flour and some olive oil."[5] Is it possible that a vegetable made its way into that pan? Absolutely. (But of course, absoluteness in context to possibility suggests the latter—most everything is absolutely possible, in other words. I digress....) Numbers 11:5 states, "We remember the fish we ate in Egypt at no cost—also the cucumbers, melons, leeks, onions, and garlic."[6] Leviticus and Numbers were likely written between 1445 and 1400 BC, describing events that most likely took place between 1445 and 1444 BC in Egypt. Some historians even claim that Egyptians were frying foods as early as 2500 BC.[7] I know humans, and if there's something to fry, we'll fry it. I'd be willing to bet dollars to fry-nuts (a donut fry) that ancient Egyptians fried vegetables.

AD 350–450: ROME

Rome boasts the world's oldest surviving cookbook,[8] the *Apicius*, likely compiled between the late fourth and early fifth centuries AD.[9] The *Apicius* has a recipe for fried chicken that includes fried vegetables: "Start to fry chicken and season with a mixtures of *liquamen* [fermented fish sauce] and oil, together with bunches of dill, leek, *saturei* [a spice plant native to southern Europe], and fresh coriander."[10] I found no evidence that any of the aforementioned vegetables were sliced. But if Julius Caesar's death taught us anything, it's that Romans were great slicers.

This piece by Jim Bachor was inspired by mosaics recently uncovered in the ancient Roman city Ostia. While this type of fryer did not exist at that time, Ostia archaeologists have unearthed large clay jars sunk into a cafe floor that could have been the first fryer.

AD 1438–1533: CHILE & PERU

Potatoes came before fries—no argument exists here—and
Chile and Peru both grew and domesticated potatoes long
before other countries did.[11] Archaeological evidence
indicates that edible potatoes were cultivated in the Andes
12,500 years ago.[12] Archaeologists have found *chuño*, freeze-
dried and then sun-roasted potatoes, from the first century
BC,[13] but to the best of my research, potatoes used in *chuño*
weren't and aren't cut, thus failing to meet our contemporary
fry definition. It seems more probable that sliced taters made
their way into *pachamanca*, an Andean dish consisting of
lamb, mutton, pork, chicken, and/or guinea pig and vegetables
marinated in spices and then cooked in a *huatia* (an earthen
oven), during the Inca Empire. If so, the Andean fry predated
the European fry by a few hundred years.

AD 1600–1700: SPAIN & PORTUGAL

The Spanish stole—among other things, like gold and lives—
the potato and possibly the sweet potato from the Incas and
brought them back to Europe. Records of both were found
in the Canary Islands in 1556.[14] Spanish and Portuguese
missionaries were also tempura frying around that time;[15]
thus, it's possible sliced taters (or other vegetables) were
tempura fried, though I found no evidence to support this.
Some claim the first recipe for fries appeared in Galicia
(northwest Spain),[16] though I found no evidence to support

that either. Even the former curator and founder of the Frietmuseum in Bruges, Belgium, Paul Ilegems, believes that Saint Teresa of Ávila fried the first potatoes in the Mediterranean region shared by Spain and Portugal.[17] If proved true, it would place Spain's and Portugal's claims one hundred to two hundred years ahead of those of their European counterparts Belgium and France. Neither Spain nor Portugal, however, appears eager to stake these claims.

AD 1680–1780: BELGIUM

Conjecture and consumption are certainly on the side of the Belgians. They assert—I say "they" because it was a Belgian journalist, Jo Gérard, who made the (uncorroborated) assertion—that sliced potatoes were being fried alongside fish in the Meuse Valley between Dinant and Liège in the late 1600s, predating the French assertion by three quarters to a full century.[18] The Belgians also contend that we dumb Americans mistakenly gave french fries their ubiquitous title, confusing French-speaking Belgian soldiers holding delicious fried esculents with French-speaking French soldiers during the First World War. Belgium does, however, appear to consume more fries—err, *frieten* (in Dutch) or *frites* (in French)—per capita than any other country.[19] But unfortunately for the Belgians, popularity does not substantiate origin (for example, Japan, not Portugal, is more known for tempura frying today).

AD 1755–1760: FRANCE

Empirical evidence for the origins of both contemporary and classical fries resides on the French side. Paradoxically, a recipe for a contemporary fry—sliced, battered, and then fried potatoes—is found in *Les soupers de la cour*, a cookbook penned by Menon (actual name unknown) in 1755,[20] before a recipe for a classical fry appeared. Evidence for the classical fry is found in 1760 in the notebook of a doctor investigating a purported assassination attempt at a monastery in Perrecy-les-Forges, Burgundy; it roughly translates as: "We found...a silver bowl containing soup and two tin dishes, in one of which were fried beans and in the other some fried potatoes."[21] Decades after that, one of the first recipes for a classical fry—raw potatoes, sliced and then fried—is found in Thomas Jefferson's scribblings between 1801 and 1809.[22] Jefferson likely pilfered the recipe during his ambassadorship to France from 1785 to 1789; it's written in French and contains the verb *frire* (deep-fry), rather than *sauter* (pan-fry).[23] To the best of my research, the above examples are the earliest references to either the contemporary or the classical fry. But as per usual, the French easily surrendered this claim during the Iraq War, asserting the fry was indeed Belgian in origin.[24]

26

Our case: being awesome—American exceptionalism. We are exceptional at taking other countries' ideas and brandishing them as our own. Case in point: the fry. As described previously, Thomas Jefferson recorded one of the earliest known classical fry recipes. Possession is nine-tenths of the law, and possession certainly favors the thief over the dupe. The founder of Facebook is, after all, Mark Zuckerberg, not Tyler and Cameron Winklevoss. And most think Thomas Edison invented the lightbulb. It's not our fault the French were too lazy to jot down the recipe. And we certainly deserve credit for taking the fry and running with it. We gifted the world the mass-produced fry.

Chapter Two

WHERE FRIES GROW

Where you find cooking, fries can be found. Most fries are initially cooked in factories—McCain Foods (the largest producer of frozen fries worldwide) makes one in every three fries around the globe[1]—and then cooked again in homes, restaurants, or *friteries*. Fresh, hand-cut fries are made in all those places too, but those fries are less common. Regardless, you won't have to footslog into the middle of the Amazon to see where fries are grown. You'll just have to visit your neighborhood restaurant—or scale the barbed-wire fence at your nearest fry factory.

FACTORIES

J. R. Simplot—a fellow Idahoan whose ubiquitous presence in my hometown, Boise, has convinced my noggin that I've seen or hugged or smelled him on many occasions, though no such occasions can be substantiated by reality—deserves credit for founding the eponymous J. R. Simplot Company, which first invented the mass-produced fry. Two of Simplot's top agribrainiacs, Ray Dunlap and Ray Keuneman, did the actual inventing in 1948. And in 1953 the Rays developed a frying method that continuously purifies and circulates the oil, eliminating the need to fry taters in batches and thus streamlining mass production. It took another decade, however, before frozen fries got hot. Homemakers embraced them initially, but restaurants did not. Then J. R. met another Ray in 1965, Ray Kroc, and the fry universe as we knew it changed forever. Kroc was an Illinois businessman who had (allegedly somewhat unethically) acquired the McDonald's restaurant chain from its founding brothers, Richard and Maurice McDonald, a few years prior. Kroc wanted to conquer the fast-food world. Simplot wanted to conquer the fry world. And together they conquered both. McDonald's became and remains the most supersized fast-food operation in the world (and the largest buyer of potatoes in the world). Simplot became (yet no longer remains) the most supersized frozen fry operation in the world (that crown now belongs to McCain Foods).

Now, mass-produced, frozen fries are welcomed worldwide, largely for three reasons: consistency, ease of use, and cost. Consistency is ensured by plucking potatoes during peak season (fall, in most of the United States) and then properly storing them in a dark (no sunlight), damp (95 percent humidity), and cool (45 to 48 degrees Fahrenheit) facility—thus preventing entropy, that cruel vixen, from getting her witchlike hands on them—before the twenty-step process described on pages 36–37 happens.[2]

This process ensures that only the best and brightest taters are fashioned into fries. Bad taters—small, bruised, defective, ugly, stupid, temperamental, judgmental—are eliminated or reconstituted into other products. And somewhere during this process, some—not all, mind you—mass-produced fries are also coated with dextrin, sugar, breading, artificial flavors, and/or other chemicals that require a chemistry doctorate to enunciate, in order to achieve ideal color and crispiness. They're mechanically made wonders: perfect crispy esculents that even novice

cooks can prepare. Just remove them from the bag and bake or fry. Easy-peasy. And cheap. Frozen, mass-produced fries cost approximately $1.50 less per pound for peeled taters and $0.50 for skin-on taters than freshly prepared fries when factoring in the costs of goods (potatoes, oil, and labor) and yield.[3] That's a significant savings.

Given the manufacturing prowess required to produce frozen fries, a virtual oligopoly exists. Three major manufacturers account for 80 percent or more of the American market: McCain Foods, the J. R. Simplot Company, and Lamb Weston (owned by ConAgra Foods).[4] And these supersized (I promise that's the last time I'll use this adjective) agribusinesses are constantly taking bites out of one another's business. A few farthings per pound is often the difference between winning a contract or not; those farthings add up quickly when contracts are for millions and millions of pounds. Together, these companies have helped create the most popular fast-food item in America.[5]

Unfortunately, mass-produced fries have contributed to bad agricultural practices in proportion to their popularity. Farmers often embrace these bad practices in order to remain competitive. Proper crop rotation gets replaced by continuous planting of single-crop fields. Manual by mechanical. Small by massive. Organic by chemical. Natural by genetically modified. These practices create a vicious cycle of dependency. Farmers rely on biotech companies and agribusinesses for the seeds to plant and the chemicals to spray to increase yields and decrease prices. Agribusinesses

20 STEPS FOR MASS-PRODUCED FRIES

(steps vary by manufacturer)

1. Potatoes are plucked during peak season.

2. Potatoes are transported to a factory.

3. Potatoes are stored in a dark, temperature-controlled warehouse.

4. Potatoes are dropped onto rollers, which remove foreign matter such as dirt, rocks, plant parts, and the eyes of the potatoes.

5. Potatoes are washed with water jets in a revolving cage.

6. Potatoes are conveyed to a sorting machine that divides potatoes by size.

7. Potatoes are collected in bins.

8. Bins open, and potatoes are dropped into steamers.

9. Potatoes are conveyed from steamer to peeler, where large, rolling bristles remove skin.

10. Skinless potatoes are conveyed to workers who inspect and remove green or rotten potatoes.

11. Potatoes are sliced by either a rotatory cutter or a hydraulic system (running water that forces potatoes through cutting blades).

12 Pieces are passed by a camera and computer; those of substandard size are flagged and blown off the production line.

13 The good pieces are dropped into a water tank to remove sugar from the flesh of the potato.

14 Pieces are blanched: first cooked in hot water and then shocked in cold water.

15 Pieces are fried in oil for approximately two minutes.

16 Excess oil is knocked off on a grated conveyor belt.

17 Fries are passed through a freezer until frozen, which takes approximately ten minutes.

18 Fries are deposited by an oscillating conveyor into chutes; each chute has a built-in scale set to the package weight.

19 Fries are dropped into plastic bags and sealed.

20 Fries are stored frozen and then shipped across the world.

want cheap taters so they can sell cheap fries. Yet less than 2 percent of the price of a mass-produced fry returns to the farmer, which has driven many farmers, especially the small guys, out of business; Idaho alone has lost over half its potato farmers in the past three decades.[6]

It's easy and obvious to blame big, ugly agribusinesses for the demise of the small, idyllic farm. Agribusinesses and biotech companies are broad-side-of-the-barn targets. The economics major, free-market proselytizer, and businessperson in me, in contrast, wants to blame consumers. Econ 101 teaches us that consumers drive commodity prices, right? Supply and demand—if the consumers want cheap fries, then golly gee goshdarnit, they'll get cheap fries. Retailers, restaurants, wholesalers, importers, brokers, manufacturers—the entire vertical supply chain—can only respond to their whimsy. Toss in government subsidies—direct subsidies, crop insurance, conservation subsidies, marketing loans, disaster aid, trade barriers, commodity price supports, production controls, et cetera—and the influence of a plethora of commodity interest groups, and the blame gets even more difficult to assign. Basic supply-and-demand principles don't seem to apply; chicken-versus-egg economic principles seem more appropriate.

Until all the links in the industrial food chain, from businesses to consumers to the government, change their practices, small farmers remain at risk. The good news for small farmers and their supporters, however, is that things are indeed changing. The number of small farms rose between 2002 and 2007 for the first time since the US Great Depression. That's mostly attributable to the local and organic food movements. The US organic market is expected to exceed a 14 percent compound annual growth rate until 2018.[8] Yet despite these gains, as of the last US Department of Agriculture's Census of Agriculture in 2012, small farms (those with less than $250,000 in annual sales) account for less than 12 percent of total agriculture production, and organic farms account for less than 1 percent.[9] In my chin of the forest, the Northwest (contrary to popular belief, Idaho is in the Northwest, not the Midwest), more and more restaurants are supporting local, organic, and small farmers, in response to customer demand.* Agribusinesses aren't, of course, blind to the trend. Lamb Weston now has an entire line, Alexia, of organic, trans fat–free, and GMO-free fries.

Small farms must tow uphill both ways to compete with supersized (I lied) farms. While I'm tempted to make a quasi-intelligible economic argument about why a large number of small farms is better for the economy than a small number of large farms, I've digressed enough.

I do feel, however, that a place exists in the freezer for mass-produced fries. I'd just like to see those fries cleaned up a bit. No chemicals and other crap. Just potatoes. Pure

---

*BFC is proud to partner with Mike Heath, of M & M Heath Farms, an organic farmer doing it the right way—and the hero of Michael Pollan's *The Botany of Desire*!

and simple. Unadulterated frozen food can taste as good and be as healthy as fresh food; ultimately, quality dictates the taste and nutrients. While I still may not buy mass-produced fries at restaurants—I prefer hands, not machines, making my food—if I ever find myself stranded on a desert island with nothing but frozen fries, peanut oil, and a solar-powered fryer, I don't think I'd starve myself. At least not for more than a few days.

HOMES

Fries are a common side dish at home. My mother often baked crinkle-cut fries to accompany burgers and corn dogs, among other dishes. While it was clear to me, even at a young age, that my mom needed evening classes from Ronald McDonald University, I devoured the fries she cooked nonetheless.

I'd wager a majority of home-cooked fries are purchased from the grocery store, thus likely manufactured by McCain Foods, the J. R. Simplot Company, or Lamb Weston. That's not because people are lazy. It's because most American households aren't equipped for frying; fryers are dangerous and uncommon household appliances. Therefore, oven-baked frozen fries are the popular choice for home cooking. Frozen fries come in just about every shape imaginable these days, from Tater Tots to RibCuts to Bent Arm Ale Craft Beer Battered Sidewinders.

RESTAURANTS

While most households bake fries, most restaurants fry fries. Commercial fryers are necessary weapons in the restaurant arsenal, and the General of Side Dishes (who wants to be the General of All Dishes) could not have risen through the ranks without an army of fryers. At one point in the history of restaurants, fryers were found in only about 10 percent of kitchens. Now I'd wager they're in every other kitchen.

Restaurants began serving hand-cut fries in the early twentieth century. Then, beginning in the late 1940s, restaurants, especially of the fast-food variety, began switching to mass-produced fries. Soggy fries knock stars off a restaurant's review, and the additional labor necessary to hand cut fries knocks off profit from a restaurant's bottom line. More recently, however, thanks to increasing awareness of the ills of processed foods and customer demand for fresh food, more and more restaurants are U-turning to the hand-cut route, taking risks with temperamental veggies and creating better, healthier, and more creative fry options.

FRITERIES

Friterie and *friture*, *baraque à frites*, *frituur*, *fritkot*, *frietkoten*, fry cart, and chip shop, among others, are general and (arguably) interchangeable terms for businesses that primarily make and serve fries, including restaurants, kiosks, carts, and vans. (Can a vending machine be a friterie? I

don't see why not. The Boise, Idaho, airport had fry vending machines in the 1990s. Now they're becoming commonplace in grocery stores in Brussels.)[10]

The original friteries were composed of not much more than pots and fry cooks, situated near busy corners, town squares, and historic sites. As with the fry itself, both the Belgians and the French claim the original friteries. In this case, I found more evidence for the Belgian argument. A serendipitously named Mr. Fritz began marketing and presumably selling (the latter being more difficult to prove) fries as early as 1849 at fairs in Liège;[11] in 1863 his widow placed an advertisement in the *Bruges Gazette* to sell fries at the newspaper's annual fair. In 1880 Benoni Pattijn sold fries on the 't Zand Square in a retrofitted hot-dog cart,[12] and in 1893 the journal *L'omnibus illustré* published an illustration of a fry merchant in Antwerp. The French claim that friteries originated near the Pont Neuf as early as 1789,[13] though I found less evidence to substantiate this claim. I did find that *La marchande de frites* by Charles Genty (see page 120) was painted in Paris in 1895, thereby suggesting that friteries existed in France by that time—gobs of photos of French friteries can be found dating to just after 1895. Regardless, friteries were common in both countries by the dawn of the twentieth century, and they spread to other countries soon thereafter. Belgium, by my back-of-the-envelope calculations, currently has the most friteries per capita, at roughly one friterie for every five thousand citizens.

45

Chapter Three

TYPES OF FRIES

& ACCOMPANIMENTS

The number of fry variations is as infinite as the imagination. The three big players in American fry production (McCain Foods, the J. R. Simplot Company, and Lamb Weston) each offer one-hundred-plus frozen varieties alone. I covered as many varieties as I had patience for below. At some point, however, even to me, the differentiations begin to blur.

SHAPES

Disclaimer: shapes cross categories. You can have a straight-cut steak fry or a crinkle-cut wedge for example. I've attempted to place each shape in its most obvious category and have listed common names as well as specific brands.

Regular (straight-cut, classic, trim, entrée-cut, fast-food; Long Branch Fries, Platter Fries, Tater Pals): The McDonald's-style fry (since McDonald's deserves credit for popularizing this width and style—and fries in general). Typically about a quarter-inch thick. Regular-cut is the most regular cut of fries.

Steak (thick, steakhouse, home-style, house, plate, diamond-cut): Any square-cut fry bigger than a regular-cut. About a half-inch thick or thicker. Red Robin serves steak fries.

Shoestring (thin, sticks/stix, shreds, juliennes; Hi-Fries, Megacrunch): Any square-cut fry thinner than a regular-cut. Popular at restaurants likely to have velvet on their walls.

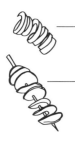

Curly (loops, spirals; Golden Twirls QQQ's, Twister): Goldilocks fries. Often breaded, coated, and/or seasoned, like Arby's fries.

Tornado (twister, hurricane; Sidewinders, Tornado Fries): Typically served on a two-foot-long wooden skewer. Popular in South Korea.

Waffle (lattice, crisscross; Cross Trax): Chick-fil-A–style fries. Like curly fries, waffle fries are often breaded, coated, and/or seasoned. CrissCut fries at Carl's Jr. are waffle fries.

Wedge (deli-cut, deli wedges, halves, jojos; Krunchie Wedges, Pinwheel Wedges, Tater-Babies, TaterDaddies): Think apple slices. Or an eighth of a sphere. Or a rounded triangular shape. A wedge, in other words.

Cube (diced, chunks, chopped, skillet, hash browns, country-style; Breakfast Cubes, CrispyCubes): While the cube is the most common shape in this category, most any geometric variation that's the size of a Ping-Pong ball or smaller fits into this group.

Chip (not the British style, which are typically steak- or wedge-cuts): Sliced flat and thin—with next to no vegetable on the inside, in other words—and served hot. Typically circular or oval, though square or rectangular certainly suffices.

Ribbon: The love child of the tornado fry and the chip. Look like ribbons, really.

Puff (puffed potatoes, pommes soufflé, soufflé potatoes): A difficult fry to make, and thus likely the rarest shape on this list. It's essentially a twice-fried, puffed-up potato chip. A balloon chip. Crispy on the outside, hollow on the inside.

Skin (shells, boats; MunchSkins): Slaughter a tater by cutting it in half, scooping out the guts, and then frying the shells. It's basically a concave, skin-on chip.

Crinkle (ridge; Colossal Crinkles, Concertinas, RibCuts, WaveLength): Groovy, groovy fries.

Slice (rounds, cottage fries, home fries, chips; Diner Slices): Sliced flat and fat, thus leaving an appreciable amount of vegetable on the inside. The hockey puck of fries.

Hash brown (patties, pancakes, shredded browns, side o' browns; Fast Browns, Golden Patties, Hash Brown Stix, Home Browns, Tri-Patties): Reconstituted, often shredded or mashed, and then formed. Typically flat and rectangular.

Mini hash brown (country hash browns, potato bites; asian moonz, Batter Bites, Harvest Splendor Bites, Old European Potato

Pancakes, Po' Balls, Puf-Ettes, Spud Bites, Spud Puppies, Tater Bucks, Tater Gems, Tater Puffs, Tater Roundabouts, Tater Sticks, Tater Tots, Tri-Taters): Reconstituted, often shredded or mashed, and then formed. Typically cubical, cylindrical, or spherical. Ping-Pong ball size or smaller.

 — **Miscellaneous** (random, DIY, the fries you didn't intend to make; Alphatots, Smiles, Starz, Stuffed Spudz): Any shape not listed above.

VEGETABLES

Potatoes. This starchy, sturdy tuber from the Solanaceae (nightshade) produces the majority of the fries in the world. According to the US Department of Agriculture, potatoes are the leading vegetable crop in the United States, contributing about 15 percent of farm sales receipts for vegetables. More than 50 percent of those sales are to processors of fries, chips, dehydrated products, and other potato miscellany; the remainder are sold fresh.[1] A good chunk of the fresh potatoes are made into fries as well.

The potato has thousands of varietals (four hundred distinct varietals are grown in the Andes alone).[2] And having more rigidity and starch than the average vegetable, the potato can be fashioned and then fried into countless shapes. Hence, if I'm doing my math correctly, which I'm sure I'm

not, approximately a gazillion different fries can, and hopefully will, be made from taters.

Most fries in the United States start as a common russet potato cultivar, led by the ever-popular russet Burbank (botanist, horticulturist, and potato entrepreneur Luther Burbank, who developed this cultivar, was nicknamed "the Wizard of Horticulture"). Russets look the potato part. They are what you think of when you think of potatoes. They also taste the part, having lower sugar and moisture and higher starch and potatoey flavor than other spuds. When they're prepped correctly, they make a light, fluffy, and crispy fry. McDonald's uses russets.

White cultivars are the second-most-popular fry potatoes in the United States. Whites generally have lower starch, lighter skin, and whiter and creamier flesh than russets. They also fry slightly whiter than other potato varieties. Whites are popular in California, the upper Midwest, and the East Coast. In-N-Out Burger uses Kennebec potatoes, a white cultivar, for its delicious hand-cut fries.

Russets and whites have been around for more than a century; golds are the new fries on the block. The Yukon Gold, the cultivar's lead singer, has been around for only a few decades. Its increasing popularity is no fad. In this fry cook's opinion, golds make better fries than russets and whites. They're golden on the outside and inside, and in your mouth they're nice 'n' crispy 'n' buttery. They also most closely resemble the Bintje cultivar, Europe's top choice for making fries and the most widely grown yellow-fleshed spud in the world.

Red and purple cultivars are climbing the fry charts as well—and for good reasons. Both offer flavor advantages and distinctions. Advantages: texture. Reds and purples, given their slightly higher starch and moisture content, tend to remain creamier on the inside post-frying. Distinctions: nuttiness. I have the opposite of a nut allergy. I'm partisan for potatoes, and I have a proclivity for nutty taters. That doesn't automatically mean that nutty taters are the best for making fries—but it does mean that, as far as I'm concerned, All Blue heirloom potatoes, of the Purple Peruvian variety, make the best fries.

Potatoes have a peculiar history. Long thought to cause leprosy, syphilis, narcosis, sterility, and general immorality (and one can argue the latter is still true, especially when fried in duck fat), potatoes were first used as animal petroleum, food energy for llamas and pigs, among others. Then the Incas figured out how to cultivate potatoes for us humans. Agronomists and anthropologists have confirmed that the Inca Empire was built by and bound to the potato;[3] the same could be said of Irish culture centuries later. That's partly because potatoes are inexpensive to grow and are close to the perfect food, one of the best all-inclusive nutritional packages—if not the very best—in the edible plant kingdom.

Growing taters, however, much like frying them, is no easy task; it takes a little science, a little luck, and a little skill. Potatoes are asexual clones—no Mr. and Mrs. Potato, in other words. They propagate vegetatively. Growers place actual pieces of the potato in the ground, not seeds (potatoes seed, but they don't naturally produce seeds). From there begins a process that I like to imagine is similar to the transformation of a mutant superhero. Buds grow from eyes. Buds metamorphose into stems, technically known as stolons. Parts of the stolons break off. These grotesque parts engorge, becoming potatoes, and then are dug from the earth, separated from their parent-self, and eventually consumed. Yum, yum.

Potatoes are also inherently wild and toxic and easily succumb to disease (organic potatoes from properly rotated crops, that is; New Leaf, Innate, and other bioengineered wonder potatoes can not only remain domesticated but also fend off disease and recite the Gettysburg Address backward). Over a few years, a once-cultivated potato can rebel, reverting to its natural, wild state. Taters are like teenagers in that way, and even the best parents—ones who aren't dousing their children with chemicals—struggle to control wild children. As noted by food writer Michael Pollan, "Nature has always exercised a kind of veto over what culture can do with a potato."[4]

Even after proper cultivation, toxins remain. The Solanaceae family, which also includes peppers and tobacco, produces solanine and chaconine, two toxic alkaloids that can cause diarrhea, nausea, cramping, headaches, and, in rare cases, organ failure and death. Potatoes therefore must be cooked to remove their toxins and release their earthy goodness.

Potatoes are low in sodium and high in potassium and fiber, contain little to no fat and cholesterol, and are loaded with vitamin C, vitamin B6, folic acid, beta-carotene, iron, and other antioxidants.[5] They're also 79 percent water (a fact I've used to convince myself that I don't need to drink water). Yet potatoes have been lambasted during the low-fat and low-carbohydrate crusades of the past few decades. Since they're high in carbohydrates—often ranked at or near the top of carbohydrate charts[6]—and sop up fats indiscriminately, fries have borne the brunt of the crusaders' vitriol.

But times are a-changin'. Scientists and society are becoming more aware of the difference between good (slow and complex) and bad (fast and simple) carbohydrates and between good (unsaturated and saturated) and bad (trans) fats.[7] In this fry cook's incredibly biased opinion, if a sliced tater isn't fried in an unhealthy fat or drenched with chemicals, preservatives, and/or bad carbohydrates (like many frozen fries), it can be healthy. Heck, I even found a study from the Department of Public Health at the University of Parma, Italy, that discovered that deep-fried potatoes have more antioxidants than potatoes cooked by other methods.[8] I'm sure I could find other studies that prove the opposite, however. Diet trends and research change, and change often. It's likely everything stated in this paragraph will be outdated by the time this book is printed. Regardless, most everything is good in moderation. Fries won't foil your diet, in other words.

Sweet Potatoes. The sweet, starchy, and sturdy tubers from the Convolvulaceae (morning glory) family are second only to taters in achieving their childhood dreams of becoming fries. While not related to the potato, the sweet potato shares a finger short of a handful of traits with taters: being a root vegetable, being hearty, being starchy, and being awesome. One of the main differences between sweet potatoes and potatoes is in the name: sweet. Sweet potatoes have almost 3.5 more grams of sugar (per 100 grams) than potatoes. This difference makes sweet potato fries difficult to make. Ask chefs and wannabe chefs alike: sweet potato fries are twice, no thrice, perhaps infinitice times more inclined to be soggy.

When on the outside of fries, sugars assist with crispiness through caramelization. When on the inside, sugars cause gelatinization—gooeyness. That, coupled with a lower starch content (approximately 45 percent less than that of taters), makes sweets difficult to crisp up. To circumvent this issue, the mass producers and their mad tater scientists have developed sorcery that regulates the sugar content of sweet potatoes to ensure ideal crispiness. In addition, the mass producers use flour and/or cornstarch and/or other stuff to further ensure crispiness (as most home-cooking recipes also recommend). That crispness you're tasting (or is it feeling?) is usually attributable to the coating, not the vegetable. But, of course, as discussed below, coatings can and often do enhance fries.

Despite the crispiness complications, sweet potato fries are rapidly increasing in popularity. Ten years ago it

was difficult to find them outside a handful of diners in the South. Now it'd be difficult not to find them. McCain Foods claims its sweet potato fries' sales have doubled since 2011.[9] Lamb Weston reports that sweet potato fries accounted for nearly 80 percent of total fry growth in 2013, and that more than 60% of consumers prefer a savory sweet potato flavor.[10] Some of this is certainly attributable to other diet trends, but most of it is attributable to fries. Orange (confusingly called "yams") and yellow (commonly called "sweet potatoes") finish first and second respectively in the sweet potato fry race. (True yams, from the Dioscoreaceae family, are unrelated to sweet potatoes and are starchier and drier.) Purple sweet potatoes, such as the Okinawa, take a distant third place.

Other Tubers. Tubers—both stem tubers (like potatoes) and root tubers (like sweet potatoes)—are generally hardier and starchier than other vegetables, making them a wee bit easier to fashion into fries. Other stem tubers, such as Jerusalem artichokes, sunchokes, and ocas, and root tubers, such as ginger, cassavas, yuccas, rutabagas, and turnips, can and should become fries.

Other Vegetables. Most vegetables are just too dainty to withstand the rigors of frying; they disintegrate or become limp and soggy, which evinces fry weakness. If given armor, however—coatings ranging from cornstarch to xanthan gum—vegetables stiffen and brave up. Then they can seize salt and submerge in sauce. Of those vegetables that match the botanist's definition, beets, artichokes, broccoli, okra, asparagus, and onions have all been coated and shaped into fries (on that note, onion rings, while a distinct commodity like chips and hash browns, are, by the contemporary fry definition, just circular fries). A coating isn't always necessary to make vegetable fries, however. BFC fries brussels sprouts straight up, for example, and then serves them with maple bacon jam.

COOKING FATS

When picking a cooking fat, you should consider the following characteristics: smoke point, flavor, diet preferences, and the texture it creates for the fries. Smoke point is the temperature at which the fat gives up on life (breaks down) and starts smoking, which not only negatively affects flavor but also increases combustibility (the point where it creates ignitable gases: the flash point). Deep-frying requires a smoke point above 360 degrees Fahrenheit, which eliminates common fats such at extra-virgin olive oil (whose smoke point is 325 degrees Fahrenheit) and unrefined butter (350 degrees Fahrenheit; butter can, however, be blended with vegetable oil to raise the smoke point).

Vegetable oils, such as canola, peanut, and sunflower, and animal fats, such as lard and beef tallow, all have high-enough smoke points to cook fries. Vegetable oils are higher in unsaturated fats and lower in flavor; veggie-oil fries have a clean flavor (more vegetable and less fat) and crispy texture

(the crispiness will, however, diminish soon after frying). Animal fats are higher in both saturated fat and flavor; animal fat gives fries a rich flavor (more fat and less vegetable) and a thin, crispy crust (which tends to stay crispy even after the fry begins to cool). For most of its fries, BFC recently switched to sunflower oil, which makes clean, GMO-free vegan fries. We also serve the Bourgeois, a russet potato fried in duck fat and sprinkled with truffle salt, which is my personal favorite.

COATINGS

Coating (breading, battering, seasoning) allows most anything to upgrade to a fry. Cornstarch, flour, sugar, and bread crumbs are common coatings. Coatings also typically include seasonings.* Sugar and/or sugar solutions regularly coat fries to enhance color, not sweetness; consumers like golden-brown fries, and sugar caramelizes the outside of russet and white potato fries. Browning does occur naturally

---

*Arby's famous curly potato fries are coated with enriched bleached flour (wheat flour, niacin, reduced iron, thiamine mononitrate, riboflavin, folic acid), salt, cornstarch, onion powder, yellow corn-meal, spices, garlic powder, leavening (sodium acid pyrophosphate, sodium bicarbonate), modified cornstarch, dextrose, spice and coloring, natural flavor, dried torula yeast, xanthan gum, sodium acid pyrophosphate, and various oils—which makes one question how much potato is under there.

in potatoes as well; potato starch eventually converts to sugar. That sugar will caramelize on the outside of a fry, but it will also gelatinize on the inside, creating a mushy yet golden fry.[†] Coatings enhance color, flavor, and crispiness. With heavily coated fries, the vegetable becomes just a conduit for the coatings.

FRY COMPANIONS

I admit it: I'm not a fry purist. I need more than vegetable and oil. Chemicals and other nonsense: no, thank you. Salt and sauce: yes, please. Fries need companions, in other words. Without companions, fries are like hot dogs without buns and mustard, or pancakes without peanut butter and maple syrup (trust me on this): good, but not as good.

[†] Browning also happens during frying through the Maillard reaction, a nonenzymatic reaction between amino acids and reducing sugars that gives food its brown color and cooked taste. In frying, however, the Maillard reaction has been linked to the cancer-causing compound acrylamide. Yowzers. But, as I'm sure you've already realized, soaking potatoes in vinegar before frying lowers the pH and blocks the nucleophilic addition of the amino acid asparagine, and thereby reduces the sugar carbonyl compound, thus preventing the formation of the corresponding Schiff base, a key intermediate in the Maillard reaction and in the formation of acrylamide. (Lauren S. Jackson and Fadwa Al-Taher, "Effects of Consumer Food Preparation on Acrylamide Formation," *Chemistry and Safety of Acrylamide in Food* 561 [2005]: 448–65.)

Salt. Few of us in recent generations have used salt outside of a shaker. Yet for the millennia before air conditioning relegated it to a garnish, salt played a much more prominent role in the daily lives of citizens and civilizations alike. It's the most important food additive in human history. Some even argue the entire foundation for human society lies on a bed of salt.[11] Homer (the poet, not Simpson) called it "the divine substance."

Salting predated frying by thousands of years. Salt preserved food and mummies as early as 6050 BC; it was first recorded in the *Peng-Tzao-Kan-Mu*, the earliest known treatise on pharmacology, as early 2700 BC.[12] Salt's history is far too long to relate in detail, but let's just say a lot of salt happened. Empires have risen from salt mines and through salt taxes. Wars (actual wars, not wars of words like the dustup over fry nomenclature described in Chapter Five) have been fought over—and won with—salt, which cures meats, treats wounds, and even sustains horses. Other fun historical uses of salt include: as currency (the word *salary* is derived from *sal*, the Latin word for "salt"), to enhance fertility, and to bring zombies back to life (this does not actually work).[13] The modern salt industry claims more than fourteen thousand different uses for salt.[14]

And salt is the most important fry additive in human history. The *Journal of Neuroscience* even has inferred that we—humans that is, though the study was conducted on hypernatremic (oversalted) rats—enjoy fries primarily

because of salt, as salt lowers stress hormones and raises oxytocin, the hormone linked to love.[15]

Salt is found in nearly every crevice of the earth and is typically harvested by one of three ways: deep-shaft mining, solution mining, or solar evaporation—producing rock salt, table salt, or sea salt, respectively. Thousands of salt varieties exist. *Fleur de sel* ("flower of salt"), *sel gris* (gray salt), flake salt, flavored and/or infused salt, smoked salt, Himalayan salt, Hawaiian sea salt, and Shio salt are several of the more common varieties. Blend salt with other seasonings and powders and the varieties multiply exponentially. Your fries, our fries, humanity's fries are better with salt.

Sauce. Sauce owes its origin to salt. Sauce derives, again, from the Latin word *sal,* referring to a "brine dressing or pickle," which later evolved into the Italian and Spanish word *salsa* and French *sauce,* from which we of course get the English word *sauce.* Early sauces were simply oversalted water, or brines. Thus sauce, by evolution and definition, plays a subordinate role to salt.

Sauce, nevertheless, is foundational to the fry experience. And today, as with fries and salts, the options are too numerous to enumerate. Here are several of the most common sauces for fries:

- **Tomato ketchup.** While not the original sauce o' fries— that distinction belongs to fish brine—tomato ketchup, at least in the United States, is the standard. One of the first ketchup recipes appears alongside one of the first recorded fry recipes in Mary Randolph's *The Virginia Housewife*, published in 1824 (Mary Randolph is Thomas Jefferson's cousin. Quite the fry family!).[16] For the better part of ketchup's existence, the field has been dominated by one iconic brand, Heinz, which douses more than 50 percent of the American market.[17] Artisanal varieties and brands such as Sir Kensington's are on the rise, though. My Magic 8 Ball prognosticates Heinz's market dominance will diminish as a result. Alas. Ketchup, Heinz included, is undoubtedly the most popular sauce o' fries in the United States. Yet despite being consumed by 93 percent of Americans and found on most every restaurant table in America, ketchup is only the second most popular condiment in the United States, after mayonnaise.

- **Mayonnaise.** An emulsion of oil, egg yolks, and either vinegar or lemon juice at its most basic; baconnaise at its best. Volumewise, mayonnaise (or mayo, as the hip kids call it) is the highest-grossing condiment in the United States, eclipsing ketchup by a mere 1.2 billion dollars annually.[18] And if you include modern aioli, which has evolved into a synonym for fancy mayo (traditional aioli was made from only olive oil, salt, and garlic, which can emulsify oil), that number is higher. Mayo is the most popular fry sauce in Europe and a standard mate for Belgian frites. Mayo also might be the most popular fry sauce in the United States if you account for aioli and the fact that mayo is a base for other common sauces, such as fry sauce and ranch, and less common sauces, such as blueberry aioli and saffron mayo.

- **Fry Sauce.** One part ketchup to two parts mayo at its simplest; at its most complex, a bowl full of condiments mixed together with seasonings and other ingredients. In other words, any sauce that's not ketchup or mayonnaise. It's sometimes called special sauce, mayoketchup (primarily in Puerto Rico), or salsa golf (primarily in Argentina and surrounding countries). The Utah-based restaurant chain Arctic Circle claims to have invented fry sauce in 1948.[19] From there, it spread up yonder to Idaho, Washington, and Oregon, where it has mostly remained. I did not realize this fact until I moved from Idaho to Virginia and began demanding fry sauce, only to be slapped with looks of befuddlement and dismissal.

- **Vinegar.** Rumor has it that a jar of pickled eggs introduced vinegar to fries. No one was present for that first date; regardless, the two have enjoyed a long, happy life together. Folks who love vinegar on their fries *love* vinegar on their fries—Swiss-style neutrality doesn't exist. While vinegar—both the more traditional white and recent malt varieties—has its fair shake of zealots in the United States, it is a more prominent sauce o' fries in Europe. However, the world's foremost fry consumers—the Belgians and the Dutch—don't favor it as much as the British and Irish do.

- **Poutine.** This Canadian concoction of hot gravy and cheese curds was invented to prevent Canadians from freezing into the tundra during their ten-month winter. Simultaneously invented by every community in Quebec in 1950-something, poutine is nearly as omni-present in Canada as ketchup is in America. It's even trickled across borders and is now readily available in the northern United States and parts of the United Kingdom. (As an odd aside, George W. Bush was once tricked into calling the Canadian prime minister "Jean Poutine.")

- **Almost-as-popular sauces:** gravy, mustard, ranch, béarnaise, hollandaise, piccalilli, chili sauce, sugared butter, satay sauce, ice cream, sour cream and onion dip, ginger-sesame sauce, olive tapenade, roasted red pepper and walnut dip, and cannabis sauce (in Amsterdam).

Other toppings. What can't you put on fries? Depends on your stomach and will to live, I suppose. Seriously. Try to think of a food item that wouldn't taste somewhat appealing as a topping for fries. Email me at fries@papress.com with your answers. Perhaps we'll include it in the next edition of this book.

While most any food thing goes, fries have their preferences. Lately, that's been a fresh dusting of bulbs and herbs (garlic, onions, shallots, chives, rosemary, thyme, oregano, basil, sage, fennel, dill, cilantro, parsley, et cetera) and cheese (Parmesan, cheddar, Pecorino, American, Romano, blue, et cetera). Lardo in Portland, Oregon, serves "dirty fries" topped with fried rosemary, peppers, lardons, and Parmesan. Orgies of ingredients (cheese, chili, grilled onions, grilled peppers, lettuce, tomatoes, olives, beef, bacon, eggs, you name it) have slept together atop beds of fries. Loaded fries, as they're colloquially hailed, are rumored to have originated in the 1950s alongside Cheez Whiz. I would've loved, just loved, to have been present for the moment that some culinary prodigy discovered that fries, Cheez Whiz, and whatever else you goshdarn please create an extraordinary (if chancy) meal.

FRY PAIRINGS

As I hope to demonstrate, fries can and should stand on their own. For too long have they been literally propped against other foods. Yet even if we can stand on our own, who doesn't like having someone stand by his or her side occasionally? (Cue "Stand by Me" by Ben E. King.)

Burgers and hot dogs are obvious companions. If you ordered either one at a restaurant and it came with a side of rice, you'd toss said rice at your server, hop on your table, scream nonsensical obscenities into the restaurant sphere, and then dive off your table and into an existential crisis. I even get upset when potato chips—or, God take me now, salads!—accompany burgers. Sandwiches are fries' next-best companions. Hot or cold. Thick-sliced, peppery pastrami (or corned beef) stacked mountainously between layers of sauerkraut, Russian dressing, Swiss cheese, and rye is my preference, but I'd take peanut butter and jelly. Fried meats, including but not limited to fish, turkey legs, chicken, and beef or pork sticks, are also common fry companions in Europe, as are meatballs, sausages, mussels, and stews. Fried anything goes in America. Steaks and tartare are common across continents—couple steak with fries and even us simpleminded Americans will call them *frites*.

Beer, in this craft beer lover's opinion, is also a fry's best buddy, more so than other drinks. Wine and fries? Yes, when pressed. Milk? I suppose. Beer, like salt, has a longer and more distinguished history than fries—possibly dating back to the early Neolithic era, around 9500 BC. Some archaeologists have even credited the "gathering" part of "hunting and gathering" to making beer.[20] Today, beer is the most widely consumed alcoholic beverage in the world and the third-most-popular drink overall, lagging behind only water and tea. The brands and varieties of beer are also endless and delicious these days. Every fry has its beer soulmate. Try a Sam Smith's Organic Chocolate Stout with a sweet potato fry sprinkled with vanilla salt and dipped in marshmallow sauce if you don't believe me.

That's my hand and those were my fries! The fries lasted
forty-three seconds. The hand is still with me.

MARTINI BIANCO ROYALE € ......
MARTINI ROSATO ROYALE € ......

you can
eat your
fries inside
if you order
a drink
Free WiFi
LUCK IS AN ATTITUDE

A bar across the street from the popular Vlaams Friethuis in
Amsterdam, leaching some of its business.

Sample Menus

TRUFFLE SHOESTRING KENNEBEC FRIES
+ beef tartare + cocoa martini

HOMESTYLE YUKON GOLD FRIES
+ tacos al pastor + Mexican Coke

RUSSET FRIES *(any cut)* with FRY SAUCE
+ Chicago-style hot dog + Leafer Madness IPA

---

short rib poutine atop
PURPLE PERUVIAN FRIES
+ Moody Tongue Black Truffle Pilsner

SALT & VINEGAR CHIPS *(British-style steak fries)*
+ beer battered fish + Aperol Spritz

CREATED BY RILEY HUDDLESTON
*Corporate Executive Chef and Beverage Director,
LondonHouse Chicago*

Chapter Four

MAKING FRIES

To pass Fry Making 101, you'll need the fry-making equipment discussed below plus a baking sheet, a few rolls of paper towels, a deep-frying/candy thermometer, oil filters, a fire extinguisher, and the skin of a crocodile. You'll also need (at minimum) vegetables, cooking fat, and salt.

Get ready to fry!

FRYING UTENSILS

Cutters. A vegetable must be sliced to be a fry, at least according to the classical and contemporary fry definitions. Whole leeks don't count. Slicing requires tools (or the fingernails of a witch). Most fries are fashioned with either knives or cutters. Knives predate fry cutters by thousands of years, plus or minus a few centuries. J. E. Howell and W. A. Chamberlain patented the first potato cutter in the United States on July 10, 1900; earlier patents may have existed in other countries. Commercial fry cutters were readily available worldwide by the 1950s. Today all types of manual and automatic cutters exist—regular, wedge, steak, curly, tornado—and can be purchased anywhere from Bed Bath & Beyond to Cabela's. A mandoline also makes an excellent fry cutter, allowing even the novice fry cook to make skinny, fat, and waffle fries.

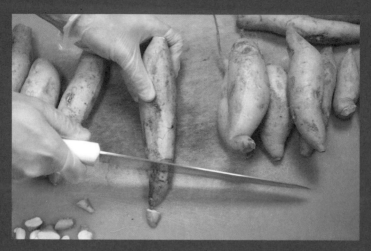

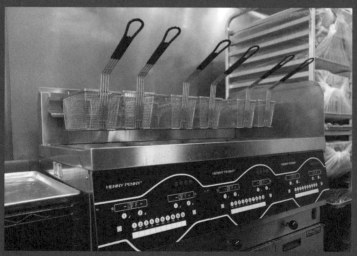

Fryers. The original fryers were pans and pots. You can still make fries in a deep pot, such as a spaghetti pot. Heck, a frying pan or wok can be used make fries. Just be warned: hot oil does not feel nearly as good on your skin as hot lotion. And be aware that it's a rather dangerous frying method—chip pan fryers, which are essentially just deep cooking pots, are the leading cause of house fires in the United Kingdom.[1]

Fryers have likely existed since the first century AD. Fast-forward almost two millennia to the 1800s, and fryers began popping up in carts, restaurants, and even households. Patents for fryer apparatuses and accessories began rising from the oil in the early 1900s. To the best of my research, the first commercial fryer, which used heating elements and a filtration system, was patented in the United States in 1918 by George L. Young on behalf of Pitco Frialator Inc., a company that still makes fantastic fryers to this day.

Commercial fryers are features of modern restaurants. They range from simple tube fryers that aren't that dissimilar from the original Pitco Frialator to complex automated fryers that can self-time, -fill, -clean, -filter, -ventilate, -raise, -lower, -regulate temperature, and -run a marathon on one leg, among other things. The fry cook's position is becoming less cook and more technician as a result.

While household fryers aren't as complex—they are constructed and operate like Crock-Pots—they are gaining popularity. By the 1950s, many residential stoves even contained embedded deep fryers. Today, countertop fryers are common in households across the United States and Europe.

Strainers. If you have a fryer, the fry basket that comes with the machine makes a great strainer. As soon as the fries are done cooking, just hold the basket above the oil and boogie. The oil will drip right off. If you're using a pot (and you're willing to risk burning your skin off), you can dump your oil and fries through a metal strainer and into another pot, though scooping the fries from the pot using a stainless-steel mesh strainer or a stainless-steel perforated spoon is a much safer idea. If properly strained and filtered after frying (you can use oil filters to sift fine particles), oil can be reused for weeks.

Tossers. Use a bowl for tossing—preferably a metal one so you can hear the fries clink, to ensure they're crispy. Tossing fries knocks off additional oil. Most fry shops use a tosser with an integrated strainer to further remove oil. The more you strain your fries, the better their chances of achieving crispiness nirvana.

Scoopers. You'll want something to scoop your fries from the tosser to wherever you're serving them from, a stainless-steel mesh strainer being this fry cook's preferred method. A hand will suffice, but only if it's coated in tungsten.

Skimmers. You'll need something to remove fry bits and food particles from the oil, which extends the life and the flavor of the oil. A stainless-steel mesh strainer is ideal here

as well. Thus, if you're counting, the same stainless-steel mesh strainer can be used for straining, scooping, and skimming: the three *s*'s.

Holders. Fries need not be held—let them be free! However, if you're inclined, you can contain fries in next to anything concave. The Belgians and Dutch hold their fries in paper cones. BFC used to serve fries that way, but we found it made salting too problematic, as our customers had to resalt every time they removed a layer of fries. Now, like Thomas Jefferson before us, we serve fries in silver bowls.[2]

91

FRY MAKING 101

Temperatures and durations for fry cooking will vary significantly, depending on the type of potato, the thickness of the cut, the oil or fat used, the time of year, the location, and the opinions of the cook and/or fry consumer. Thicker cuts, higher altitude and humidity, and out-of-season potatoes will require additional cooking time and/or higher temperatures. Trial and error is necessary.

Turn down the lights, turn up the Solomon Burke, grab a bottle of beer, and let's make some fries.

The College Freshman Fry

Buy a bag of frozen fries. Get the *CliffsNotes* for the instructions on the back of the bag. Immerse the fries in hot oil or fat. Wait for the fries to float. Scoop them out. Enjoy.

The College Senior Fry

Buy a bag of frozen fries. Know that you know the instructions on the back of the bag. Soak the fries in beer for a few minutes. Immerse the fries in hot oil or fat. Wait for the fries to float. Scoop them out. Enjoy.

The Oven Fry

Preheat your oven to 425 degrees Fahrenheit. Cut Yukon Gold potatoes any way that makes you happy; I prefer quarter-inch regular cuts. Coat the cuts with your preferred fat or oil; I prefer duck fat. Spread them on a baking sheet and place them in the oven. Bake for 30 to 35 minutes, turning occasionally. Remove them from the oven, quickly salt, and indulge.

The Classical Fry
THE GENERAL PROCESS

The steps below are for potato fries. Fries made with sweet potatoes and other vegetables require additional steps.

1. Drive to a corporate farm under the darkness of night while wearing a Batman costume. Use your grapple gun to climb over the presumably barbed-wire fence. Dig up and then steal a potato. Flee. That, or buy a potato from the grocery store.

2. Decide if you want skin-on or -off fries. Choose skin-on to save a step (and because they're healthier and better that way).

3. Cut the potato—any way that makes you smile. Cut a smiley face if you can.

4. Soak the cut potatoes in water. Soaking sucks starch from the center to the skin of the tater, helping fries get crispy and preventing them from sticking together. Some claim just a few minutes in lukewarm water works. Others claim overnight in cold water is best. I prefer the latter. (You can add vinegar to the water at this step as well, which speeds starch extraction and delays browning—helps make fries crispier, in other words.) →

5 Drain and dry the soaked cuts. Vigorous shaking will suffice. As will paper towels. You can also use an oven at a low temperature—no higher than 100 degrees Fahrenheit for no longer than 5 minutes.

6 Blanch the dried cuts. Blanching precooks and removes the bite of the starch flavor. For potatoes, there are two common blanching methods: cooking in high-temperature water (around 170 degrees Fahrenheit) or frying in low-temperature fat or oil (around 300 degrees Fahrenheit. The temperature of the water or oil will initially drop, but it should recover by the end of the frying time; the important thing is to ensure the temperature is right before the fries are dropped). The latter step is called the first or preliminary fry.

7 Cool or freeze the blanched cuts. This is, technically, part of the blanching process: heating and then immediately cooling. Cuts can be cooled on a tray until they're room temperature, in a fridge until they're cold, or in a freezer until they're frozen.

8 Heat the oil to at least 350 degrees Fahrenheit. Fry the cold cuts (the fries, not meat) again. This is called the final or finish fry.

9 Salt and sauce the fries and enjoy posthaste.

The Classical Fry
THE SPECIFIC RECIPE

1. Cut a medium-size, skin-on Kennebec (or white or russet if you can't find a Kennebec) potato into quarter-inch strips.
2. Soak the cuts in water in the fridge overnight.
3. Blanch (fry) the cuts in lard or peanut oil (I prefer lard for flavor and crispiness reasons and peanut oil for health and nuttiness reasons) at 300 degrees Fahrenheit for 4 minutes.
4. Place the cuts in the freezer until they're frozen.
5. Fry the cuts again at 360 degrees Fahrenheit for 1 minute.
6. Shake, dry, and then immediately salt and ingest the fries.

VARIATIONS

The Pancake Fry

Heat the oil or fat in your fryer or deep pot (no more than a quarter full) to 350 degrees Fahrenheit. Prepare your favorite pancake batter. Cut a vegetable any way that makes you smile. Dip the cuts in the batter. Fry (times will vary depending on the vegetable used and the thickness of the cut). Scarf.

The Belgian Fry

Search for Bintje potatoes. Search some more. Give up. Find Yukon Gold potatoes. Bintje is the favorite potato for making

Belgian fries (or should I say *frieten*?), but it's hard to find stateside. The Gold, in my opinion, is the closest potato to the Bintje likely found in your grocery store. Make sure the potatoes you select are firm (not squishy).

Peel two or three potatoes. Submerge them in a bowl of room-temperature water for 5 minutes. Heat your cooking fat in a countertop fryer (preferably) or a deep pot to 325 degrees Fahrenheit. (Note: Temperatures and cooking times will vary depending on the quality of potatoes, whether you use a fryer or a pot, and the choice of cooking fat. You'll likely need to adjust the temperature plus or minus 10 degrees and the frying time plus or minus 1 minute to get it right.)

Remove the soaked potatoes and quickly dry them. Whip out a knife. Make a crazy face just for giggles. Cut the potatoes into half-inch strips. Delicately drop the cuts into the cooking fat, avoiding splashing yourself. Fry for at least 3 minutes—or until the outside of the fry begins to bubble ever so slightly. Remove the cuts from cooking fat and place them on a baking sheet until they reach room temperature—at least 20 minutes.

Turn up the cooking fat to 360 degrees Fahrenheit. Add the cooled cuts and fry them for 1 to 2 minutes, until they're fully floating and slightly browned. Remove and quickly dry. Salt. Love yourself.

THE FRY ALGORITHM

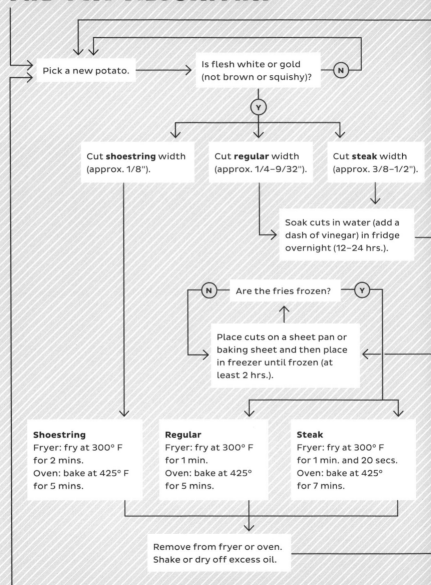

Pick a new potato. → Is flesh white or gold (not brown or squishy)? — **N**

Y

Cut **shoestring** width (approx. 1/8").

Cut **regular** width (approx. 1/4–9/32").

Cut **steak** width (approx. 3/8–1/2").

Soak cuts in water (add a dash of vinegar) in fridge overnight (12–24 hrs.).

N — Are the fries frozen? — **Y**

Place cuts on a sheet pan or baking sheet and then place in freezer until frozen (at least 2 hrs.).

Shoestring
Fryer: fry at 300° F for 2 mins.
Oven: bake at 425° F for 5 mins.

Regular
Fryer: fry at 300° F for 1 min.
Oven: bake at 425° for 5 mins.

Steak
Fryer: fry at 300° F for 1 min. and 20 secs.
Oven: bake at 425° for 7 mins.

Remove from fryer or oven. Shake or dry off excess oil.

Test blanch
a few slices.

Regular
Water: boil for ≈ 10 mins.
Oven: bake at 300° F
for 25 mins.
Fryer: fry at 300° F
for 4 mins.

Steak
Water: boil for ≈ 15 mins.
Oven: bake at 300° F
for 30 mins.
Fryer: fry at 300° F
for 4 mins.

Is starch foaming
atop the water?

Is the skin of the potato
slightly brown, slightly
bubbling, and slightly firm?

Blanch remaining cuts.

Retest cuts at +/- 1 min.
and +/- 10° F.

If undercooked, increase temperature 5–10
degrees and fry for an additional 15–30 secs.

If overcooked, start over. Sad face.

Drop fries in stainless steel
bowl. Did they clink? Are they
very crispy? Slightly brown? → *Salt and enjoy!*

Chapter Five

THE CULTURE OF FRIES

ACROSS THE GLOBE

Fries are, quite literally, all over the map (except perhaps in Tetepare). I didn't fully believe it, however, until I ate fries at a restaurant in the remote and destitute state of Odisha, India, where my wife and I adopted our precious and precocious daughter. After several weeks and bouts of giardiasis, I could no longer stomach Indian food. I was stuck inside our hotel's restaurant. It was flooding outside. I was suffering from a fry drought on the inside. I couldn't read the menu, and none of its excessively glossy photos showed any fries, so in a moment of desperation I asked the server, "Do you have fries?" His response: "Yes, either thick or skinny."

Fries are the default side dish of the Western world, found and craved most anywhere in the Americas and Europe. Fries are, somewhat officially, considered one of the national dishes of Britain and Belgium, paired with fish and mussels, respectively—and here's hoping other countries follow suit! Fries have recently begun their as-salt on the Eastern world. Fifty years ago, China was the world's fifth-largest producer of potatoes, behind the USSR, Germany, Poland, and the United States.[1] Today, China is the world's largest producer, consumer, and processor of potatoes, thanks mostly to the globalization and growth of fast food. However, in per-capita potato and fry consumption, China limps behind the West: Americans eat twice as many taters as the Chinese do,[2] and China does not crack the top ten of my McDonald's Index.*

104

Not all countries ingest or respect fries equally. Below I've listed the top ten fry countries, somewhat subjectively ranked by amalgamated consumption, history, and respect for fries in an appreciable mass. In other words, if a nation's fries are found only in global fast-food establishments, that country didn't make the list.

1. Belgium. No other country has a more storied, fanatical, and ravenous relationship with fries, boasting more fry dispensaries and consumption than any other country in the world. Belgians also respect the fry more than any other nationality. To a Belgian, the fry is not a mere side dish, something tossed haphazardly alongside other dishes simply to fill a plate. No, no, no, no. *Frites* and *frieten,* as those crazy Walloons and Flemish, respectively, call them, are the

---

* Next to no research exists on fry consumption by country beyond the frozen-fry market, so I developed the McDonald's Index as a metric (although certainly not the only possible metric) to quantify various countries' fry consumption. The index simply calculates the number of McDonald's per capita per country. McDonald's has the most popular fries in the world—and it's reasonable to infer that McDonald's-free countries don't have long-standing fry cultures. It's also reasonable to infer that if a country is high on the index, it's high in total fry consumption. The McDonald's Index is similar to the Big Mac Index produced by the *Economist* in that they both involve McDonald's and are indexes; it's dissimilar in that the McDonald's Index is erratically researched and has nothing to do with purchasing-power parity.

dish. *The* dish. The main item. Belgian frites are revered and sought after by nationals and tourists alike, more so than in any other country. And Belgian *friteries* are frite showcases, creating frite masterpieces. Twice-fried in fat, sprinkled with pixie salt, and covered with a smorgasbord of heavenly sauces: Belgian frites take the cake. Belgian frite passion also, in my opinion, lends some—though not absolute— credibility (as mentioned, popularity does not substantiate origin) to the French-vs.-Belgian fry-origin debate. As noted by the historian Roel Jacobs, the origin of french fries holds little interest. In his eyes, the more interesting subject is the manner in which fries have been adopted on both sides of the border. In France they usually come as an accompaniment to meat, whereas in Belgium they are more often eaten on their own.[3]

2. Netherlands. The Dutch love their *patat/friet/frieten* nearly as much as the Belgians love theirs, and that's not just because they share a border, history, culture, institutions, languages, family, trade, investments, sporting preferences, and security interests. Dutch *frietkot/frituur* (friteries) are nearly as common as Belgian ones. The Netherlands is the fourth-happiest country in the known cosmos,[4] and its fry consumption and appreciation certainly deserve credit for that. The Dutch delightfully and frequently submerge their fries in mayo and/or a peanut satay sauce.

3. US of A. 'Murica is the birthplace of mass-produced fries and fast food, the success of both items being inter- twined. Mass-produced fries have shrunk costs and swelled profits, allowing fast-food outlets to expand rapidly and pervasively—the number of fast-food outlets in the United States has tripled since 1970 to more than 300,000 today. McDonald's, KFC, Burger King, Wendy's, and Dairy Queen, all of which serve fries and were founded in the United States, are five of the top ten US restaurant chains with the highest global sales.[5] Fast-food fries also cleared the beach for unique and creative handmade fry options, both here and abroad. The United States has the most diversi-fried portfolio in the world, and Americans fiercely defend their fries; a 2014 Harris Poll, taken in conjunction with National French Fry Day (July 13), showed that one third of Americans would not give their last fry to their favorite celebrity.[6]

4. United Kingdom. This is the birthplace of fish and fries—*er*, chips. Bored scholars even claim that chip shops, which originated in the 1860s, were the first fast-food establishments (for comparison, the first US fast-food estab- lishments, A&W and White Castle, originated in 1919 and 1921, respectively). Fish and chips is the national dish of the United Kingdom. Malt vinegar and brown sauce, a condiment made with malt vinegar, tomatoes, tamarind, and a sundry of spices (HP Sauce, for example), are common sauces o' fries in the United Kingdom.

5. France. Perhaps France should be higher on this list. After all, the French invented *pommes frites*, right? *French* is also the adjective that most often precedes *fries*. Or perhaps I'm still tender from the verbal beating I took from a Paris Métro kiosk attendant after soliciting instructions in English on a recent trip. Whatever the case, frites don't appear to be as prominent in France as they are in the above countries. Frites do accompany many dishes and are staples in brasseries, but friteries are virtually nonexistent. On that recent trip to Paris, I sleuthed for vintage friteries, such as the one pictured, but they had either moved or gone out of business (or maybe that cranky Métro attendant intentionally misdirected me); I found only the remnants of defunct friteries. France does, however, rank sixth on the McDonald's Index, and McDonald's occupies prime Paris real estate—one is stationed in front of the Luxembourg Gardens and a few blocks from the Panthéon, for example. It makes one wonder if the French love frites but are too cool to admit it. French frites are often served with ketchup and rémoulade, a mayo-based sauce that typically includes curry, paprika, lemon juice, horseradish, and mustard.

6. Canada. Second only to the United States on the McDonald's Index, Canada has approximately one McDonald's for every 25,000 citizens. Canada is the sixth-happiest country in the world.[7] It also gifted humanity poutine, and the importance of that culinary achievement should not be understated; Canadians themselves rank poutine as the tenth-greatest

Canadian invention, bettering the electron microscope, the BlackBerry (this one makes sense), the paint roller, the caulking gun, lacrosse, Plexiglas, radio voice transmission, and basketball.[8] Canada would be higher on this list if not for my obligation to enhance the inferiority complex of our huge little cousin.

7 & 8. Australia and New Zealand. Like the British, Aussies and Kiwis enjoy vinegar on fries. Unlike the British, they scatter chicken salt on their fries.

9. Japan. This is the country that popularized tempura-frying, which can make most any vegetable into a fry. Fries in Japan are often served with *furikake*, a condiment that includes dried bonito flakes, seaweed, sesame seeds, and other seasonings.

10. Germany. Ranking last on the McDonald's Index top ten, Germany often serves fries alongside currywurst, a pork sausage topped with curry ketchup that doubles as a dip for the *pommesfrites*.

Other countries that just missed the list, less because of consumption, history, or respect, and more for the unique way they chomp fries:
Albania. *Patatis* are served lukewarm and with grease.
Bulgaria. Пържени картофки are topped with spices and *sirene*, a grated brine cheese similar to feta.

Malaysia. More than they eat regular fries (*kentang goreng*), Malaysians snack on sweet potato balls called *fan shu tan*.

Mexico. *Papas a la francesa* are served with hot sauce and lemon juice.

Namibia. Namibians call fries "slap chips."

Philippines. *Piniritong patatas* are dipped in banana ketchup.

Poland. *Frytkis* are typically served with garlic cream, garlic sauce, and/or minced garlic—garlic fries take on new meaning here.

Romania. Fries are called *cartofi prajiti* and served with *mujdei*, a thin, spicy sauce made of minced garlic cloves, salt, oil, vinegar, and water.[9]

IN POLITICS

Belgium recently broke the record for a country going the most consecutive days with no government (the previous record of 249 days was held by war-torn Iraq). The wealthier, Dutch-speaking Flemish to the north squabbled with the poorer, French-speaking Walloons to the south. The reasons are complex and confusing. Students comically protested and celebrated this record by stripping down to their skimpies and doling out free beer and frites. It became known as *De friet revolutie* or *La révolution des frites*, depending which side you're on. The shutdown ended after 340 days because of a looming financial meltdown in the eurozone. And to celebrate, you guessed it: Belgium dispensed gratis frites

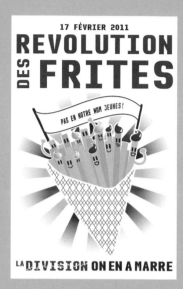

again. (Come on, Obama! We couldn't have done that to celebrate the end of our last shutdown?!)

It's not the first time fries have been caught in the crossfire of war. In 2003 the Republican chairman of the Committee on House Administration, Bob Ney, in response to France's opposition to the proposed invasion of Iraq, renamed french fries served in congressional cafeterias "freedom fries." The term spread like wild-fryer from there. Restaurants across the country embraced the term, and it was satirized by everyone from Tina Fey on *Saturday Night Live* to the character Stan on *American Dad!* It remains a pop culture joke today. At the time, I was bewildered why the United States bothered soliciting French military assistance, but I was less surprised by the freedom fries incident. Comfort food unleashes unified and unabashed patriotism. (The United States rebranded frankfurters as hot dogs during the First World War for similar reasons.)

Fries are also the food of political demigods (and perhaps regular gods). Leaders on nearly every continent have expressed their fondness for fries. Thomas Jefferson fell in love with fries during his ambassadorship to France and is widely credited with popularizing fries in the United States. Winston Churchill called fish and chips "good companions," and he ensured that neither was subject to rationing during the Second World War, out of fear that it would damage British morale. Bill Clinton often ran to McDonald's to ingest one of his favorite foods (that last statement loses some meaning, since just about every food seemed to be Clinton's favorite). Kim Jong-un, in addition to having the best hair and dictating the most closed-off country on Earth, regularly opens his doors to fries.[10] President Barack Obama often hosts staff and diplomatic meetings around plates of fries and is a regular at Five Guys Burgers and Fries.

IN POP CULTURE

One would be hard-pressed—well, perhaps soft-pressed—to find a medium of pop culture in which fries aren't featured. A complete list would be too long for this book, so I've included a few highlights below:

Small Screen. In "The Postponement" (season seven, episode two of the forever-popular sitcom *Seinfeld*), George Costanza and Jerry Seinfeld, wedged into their regular booth at Monk's Cafe, confer about how to postpone George's engagement. A strategy of calculated indifference reveals itself to George after he sees a man break up with his girl-friend and then, immune to her crying, ask, "Are you gonna eat those fries?" In another hit Seinfeld show, the web series *Comedians in Cars Getting Coffee*, fries receive prime-time attention in the episodes featuring Chris Rock and Gad Elmaleh. Cross-dressing David Spade, Adam Sandler, and Chris Farley share fries on a *Saturday Night Live* skit—Farley's character eats most of the fries. *Looney Tunes* had a "French Fries" episode, in which a plate of fries threatens Daffy Duck and Porky Pig's friendship, as well as Bugs

Bunny's chance to watch a football playoff game. Cartman and Kyle eat McDonald's fries in a hot tub full of KFC gravy in the "Crack Baby Athletic Association" episode of *South Park*. A sitcom titled *Fries with That?*, about teens mismanaging a fast-food joint, aired in Canada for a few years. Frylock, a giant, floating, anthropomorphic box of fries, is a character on the Adult Swim animated television series *Aqua Teen Hunger Force*. And, of course, culinary shows regularly showcase fries—BFC was even featured on the Food Network's *America's Best: Top Ten Comfort Foods* and the Travel Channel's *Food Paradise*, "Deep Fried Paradise 4"!

Big Screen. This scene in the film *Pulp Fiction* helped clarify the difference between how Americans and the Dutch consume fries:

> VINCENT: But you know what they put on french fries in Holland instead of ketchup?
> JULES: What?
> VINCENT: Mayonnaise.
> JULES: Goddamn!
> VINCENT: I seen 'em do it, man. They [bleepin'] drown 'em in that [stuff].

Kevin Kline stuffs fries up Michael Palin's nose in *A Fish Called Wanda*. Pregnant burger and fry cook Drew Barrymore falls for pilot Luke Wilson in *Home Fries*. Matt Damon and Greg Kinnear's characters run Quikee Burger,

What Fries Are Called

COUNTRY	LANGUAGE	WHAT FRIES ARE CALLED
Belgium	Vlaams (Flemish Dutch)	friet frieten frut (Antwerp)
Belgium	French	frites pommes frites
Brazil	Portuguese	batata frita
Bulgaria	Bulgarian	Пържени картофки
Canada (Quebec)	French	patates frites
China	Mandarin	shu tiao
Colombia	Spanish	papas a la francesa papas fritas
Czech Republic	Czech	hranolky (little prisms)
Denmark	Danish	pomfritter
Finland	Finnish	ranskalaiset perunat ranskikset (slang)
France	French	frites pommes frites
Germany	German	pommes pommesfrites
Greece	Greek	(Βελγική) πατάτες τηγανητές
Hong Kong	Cantonese	shu till
Hungary	Hungarian	sult krumpli
Indonesia	Indonesian	kentang goreng
Ireland	Gaelic	sceallóga
Israel	Hebrew	metuganim

COUNTRY	LANGUAGE	WHAT FRIES ARE CALLED
Italy	Italian	patatine fritte
Japan	Japanese	furaido poteeto furenchi furai
Korea	Korean	gamza teekim
Latvia	Latvian	(Beļģu) frī kartupeļi
Macedonia	Macedonian	(Белгискиот) картофи компири
Mexico	Spanish	papas a la francesa
Netherlands	Dutch	patat patat frites Vlaamse friet
Norway	Norwegian	pommes frites
Philippines	Filipino/Tagalog	patatas na pinirito piniritong patatas
Poland	Polish	frytkis
Portugal	Portuguese	batatas fritas
Romania	Romanian	cartofi prajiti
Russia	Russian	(Бельгийские) картофелем фри
Serbia	Serbian	(Белгијска) кромпир кромпир
Slovenia	Slovenian	(Belgijski) krompirček krompir
Spain	Spanish	patatas fritas
Sweden	Swedish	franske kartofler pommes frites strips (slang)
Thailand	Thai	man fa rang tod
Turkey	Turkish	(Belçikalı) patates kızartmas patates kizartmasi
United Kingdom	English	chips
USA	English	(french) fries

which naturally serves fries, in the Farrelly brothers' *Stuck on You*. Jonah Hill sings a song about fries in *21 Jump Street*. Pixar's recent smash hit, *Inside Out*, about five personified emotions inside the mind of a young girl, features french fries that grow as tall as sequoias in Imagination Land, a theme park located inside the heroine's head. And prominent documentaries, such as *Food, Inc.* and *Super Size Me*, have, somewhat unjustly, barbed fries—the latter even cracking *Cracked* magazine's "6 Famous Documentaries That Were Shockingly Full of Crap."[11]

Music. Toss in the slaw of French and Dutch songs about fries, such as *"Bleu, blanc, rouge et des frites"* by Marcel Amont and *"Friet met mayonaise"* by Johnny Hoes, and this list would be quite long. "Do You Want Fries with That?" by Tim McGraw, "If French Fries Were Fat Free" by Alan Jackson, "Fried Neckbones and Some Home Fries" by Santana, "Freedom Fries" by Robert Plant, "Burgers and Fries" by Charley Pride, and "Do Fries Go with That Shake" by George Clinton are a few songs by well-known artists. Fries have even wedged their way into the titles of some albums, such as *French Fries* by the Bitteroots and *Burgers & Fries* by Hotel Oscar, as well as the names of some artists, such as French Fries, a French house and techno musician; Disco Fries, an American house and electronic DJ and production duo; and Freedom Fry, a French and American indie-pop duo.

Literature. Charles Dickens wrote about "husky chips of potato, fried with some reluctant drops of oil" in *A Tale of Two Cities*. Nickelodeon produced a book called *The Eye of the Fry Cook: A Story About Getting Glasses*, in which SpongeBob SquarePants auditions for Bikini Bottom's inaugural gourmet fry-cook academy, only to discover he can't read his study cards because he needs glasses. *New York Times* best-selling author David Baldacci has written a youth series called *Freddy and the French Fries* about a genius who builds robotic shoestring, waffle, wedge, curly, and crinkle fry characters that come to life after being struck by lightning. Aquaman eats fish and chips in the comic *Aquaman #1*, and Nova flies through fries in *Nova #21*. Belgium even has *frietstrips* (fry comics), such as *Het broze barakske la baraque brinque balante*, which appears to be about a giant who loves fries.

Marketing. Fries get marketed. Fast-food companies spend two billion dollars annually on advertising (which presumably includes some fry ads), lagging behind only the automobile and pharmaceutical industries in greasing the hands of consumers.[12] According to *Advertising Age*, McDonald's is the fourth-most-advertised brand in the United States.[13] It's branded my brain. I still remember that McDonald's commercial from the nineties where the father eats his kids' fries on the way home from work—I had long suspected my father did the same thing. McDonald's ran a series of commercials during the seventies featuring the

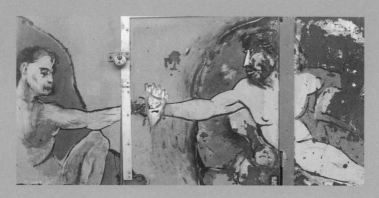

120

Fry Kids, who more closely resembled mops than they did fries. Sonic ran kids' promotions featuring the Justice League of Tater Tots. The paradoxically named New York Fries (based in Canada) ran clever billboards with the line "Vodka Is Made from Potatoes. Such a Waste" next to a picture of its fries. McDonald's had a viral marketing campaign featuring the fictional Lincoln Fry, which resembled Lincoln's profile. After the Lincoln Fry was featured in a Super Bowl XXXIX ad, it was auctioned off for charity for $75,000, making the fry second only to the *Pommes d'Or* (discussed below) in terms of monetary value. A commercial fryer company (name not disclosed) recently contacted Twitter about purchasing data tracking tweets about soggy fries so it could target its sales pitches for new fryers to restaurants tagged with soggy fries.[14] And so on.

Art. Most fry art is kind of kitschy (like this book). Some of it is pretty, like *La marchande de frites* by Charles Genty. Or *Ancient Fryer Instructions* by Jim Bachor (on page 22), which mimics mosaic tile art discovered in the ancient Roman city of Ostia (which possibly hosted the world's first fryer).[15] The McDonald's in photographer Víctor Enrich's *Medusa* (on page 123, bottom) makes it appear as if he transformed a hotel into a box of fries (though the title of the piece suggests otherwise). Fries may have also influenced John Henry's sculpture *Alachua* at the University of Florida—students actually refer to it as "French Fries from Hell." Fries certainly influenced Stefan Bohnenberger's *Pommes d'Or*, a sculpture of two gold fries—perhaps the most expensive fries in the world. (The model fries he used to make the sculpture, which had been displayed for twenty-plus years—yum, yum—went missing, and the gallery had to award Bohnenberger $2,500 in damages.) And finally, and most impressively, Sir Kensington's, the artisanal ketchup and sauce wizard, recently concocted *Fries of New York*, an exhibition showcasing New York City's incredible fry diversity though one hundred different fry specimens.

123

THE FUTURE OF FRIES

To research this fryography, I took a trip to Belgium, France, and the Netherlands. Between fry binges—I ate fries at every meal—I ventured to Antoine-Augustin Parmentier's grave in Père Lachaise Cemetery. Parmentier is widely credited with popularizing taters in France—some postulate that fries would not have been created if not for him. After squandering hours misreading the cemetery map, I eventually—and nearly literally—stumbled onto Parmentier's gravesite. Potato plants (which grow lovely flowers, by the way) surrounded the site. Nice touch, I thought. Shortly thereafter, I heard a French Yanni look-alike tell a couple of British ladies examining a nearby gravesite about the future zombies likely inhabiting it. Yanni headed in my direction after that. I was frightened. Then he said: "Potato guy, right? He gave France potatoes." He asked me why I was visiting Parmentier's grave. I told him I was writing a book on fries. Then, as he began to move toward the next tourist, he uttered this: *"N'écrivez pas les frites. Vivent les frites."* ("Don't write fries. Live fries.")*

Fries are as ubiquitous a food item as you'll find in the world. Gas stations, sporting events, restaurants, grocery stores, food trucks, vending machines—where food is consumed, fries can be found.

Many variations of fries fall outside my contemporary definition: any vegetable, cut any way imaginable, coated with anything edible, cooked any way feasible, and consumed hot. Expanding that definition to include fruit grows fry varieties exponentially. Chances are you've had a fruit fry. Zucchini, squash, okra, cucumbers (via pickles), avocados, pumpkins, and jalapeños can be served as fries—jalapeño fries dipped in regular ol' fry sauce is one of my favorite combinations. Burger King (and BFC, for that matter) also serve apple fries, which are simply raw apples sliced like fries.

Why stop at fruit, though? Finger steaks, which were invented in the Gem State (at one point, evidently, Idaho was better known for gems than for taters), are literally steak fries: pieces of steak cut frywise, coated with a tempura-like batter, and then fried. Lamb fries are just (and I say "just" with tongue in cheek) fried lamb testicles. (Curiously, the word *avocado* is derived from the Aztec word for "testicle.") Spam fries are also gaining in popularity across the United States (which does, however, raise the question of whether Spam is meat).[1]

Dessert and candy fries are also common. S'more fries, which are just as scrumptious as they sound, are roasting on restaurant menus across the country, as are donut and pancake fries. Candy fries, such as Haribo's Sauer Pommes and Oriental Trading Company's Gummy Flesh Fries, can be found in grocery stores and gas stations around the globe and make excellent illegally snuck-in movie candy.

---

*He probably didn't utter that. I don't speak French, so I jotted down, phonetically, what I thought he said in my vacation—*er*, research—notebook. I know he said "frites" twice. The rest is French to me. Regardless, the phrase stuck. I actually live fries. Many of us live fries.

HARIBO
HARIBO MACHT KINDER FROH UND ERWACHSENE EBENSO
F!ZZ
SAUER
POMMES

While we're at it, let's mention fry-shaped or -themed chips, such as Andy Capp's BBQ Fries, French's Potato Sticks, Frito-Lay's Chester's Fries, Gedilla's Fries, Herr's Potato Stix, Jack 'n Jill Roller Coaster Potato Rings, Jagabee's fry chips, Ore-Ida's Funky Fries (gone but not forgotten), Orion's O!Karto, Pik-Nik's Shoestring Potatoes, Ruffles's Crispy Fries, and Sensible Portions' Potato Straws, to name a bunch. (Of course, as we all know, chips are really just cold, inferior fries.)

Fries have become a fryrus, spreading their deliciousness to traditional entrées as well. Fry pizza? You betcha. Swap dough for fries and you have superior pizza. Fry burritos? Why not? Del Taco already figured that out—its California Burrito was even gushed over by *GQ* magazine.[2] Fry salad? Sunshine Tavern in Portland, Oregon, serves a fry salad with provolone and salami. Fry corndog? Okay.... South Koreans have figured out a way to stick fries to a stick, and they deserve an award (or at least a congratulatory handshake) for that.

And don't even get me started on novelty fry products, such as the fry phone, fry costumes, McDonald's French Fry Snack Maker, french fry finger puppets, fry dog toys, and so on....

Most anything can be a fry. At their basest, fries are cheap commodities rapidly consumed. At their best, they are culinary masterpieces goading master chefs in the never-ending pursuit of perfection.

Since just about everything can be a fry, let's ensure fries are good (we owe it to the children, after all.) Fries can be clean. Processed and genetically modified additives are unnecessary. Natural ingredients and cooking methods are at the disposal of restaurants, mass-producers, and households alike. Modernist and molecular gastronomical cooking techniques, such as *sous vide*, vacuum sealing, flash-freezing, and ultrasonic baths, are creating natural yet technologically advanced fries (though they require a mad scientist's laboratory to create).

Adam Smith (that one economist from that one econ class) regretted the lack of information that is the byproduct of free-market capitalism. Companies can't tell the entire story about their products; they must be selective—and they're incentivized to select the stories that are best for their business. I do feel businesses can do better, however, by informing customers what's in their products. They can be held accountable. Businesses need to mean what they say—not follow the example of Wendy's, which got busted for using exotic laboratory chemicals to improve its "natural" fries' appearance, flavor, and ease of cooking.[3]

Food businesses are improving in general. Lamb Weston now has an organic fry line. Cascadian Farm exclusively produces organic fries. Restaurants are making fries from better vegetables. Even McDonald's recently refused to use Simplot's genetically modified Innate potato.[4] The fry pendulum may be swinging back to organic.

Also, while we're talking about better, healthier fries, let's dispel one final myth. Fries aren't unhealthy. Yes, I said it. Fries won't kill you, despite what health fanatics and

first ladies may tell you. Fries are simply vegetables and oil.
Researchers from University of Naples Federico II and Dolce
& Salato culinary school in Italy recently proved that frying
raw potatoes once (versus using frozen fries or frying twice) is
not unhealthy—once-fried fries contain the same amount of
oil as a bowl of Neapolitan spaghetti does.[5] Science is also
beginning to dispel the myth that saturated fat consumption
is linked to heart disease.

Overconsumption and idleness are the main ill-health
culprits in the United States—not fries. Japan is first in the
world in per-capita expenditures on delivery/takeout foods[6]
and sixth on the McDonald's Index, yet it's first for longevity
and fifth for overall health. Of course, correlation doesn't
necessarily indicate causation, but an active lifestyle will keep
you healthy and allow you to have your fries and eat your
burger too.

So let's follow this argument further. If fries make us
happy and can be healthy, can they also bring about world
peace? Most definitely. Fries can fend off global warming
while fixing the energy crisis, making the world less
dependent on crude oil and preventing wars in the Middle
East. Fry oil easily recycles to biodiesel, and biodiesel can
reduce greenhouse gas emissions, pollution, biodegradation,
and deforestation. According to the US Environmental
Protection Agency's "Renewable Fuel Standards Program
Regulatory Impact Analysis," biodiesel produced from waste
grease (oils and fats) results in an 86 percent reduction in
greenhouse gases.[7] BFC is proud to partner with ReCab,

133

a Boise taxi company that runs its fleet exclusively on converted fry oil. And fries make us happy, and if everyone were a little happier, wouldn't peace be a little easier? As stated by Paul Abrahamian, who co-owns Sticky's Finger Joint in New York City, "The french fry should be the global symbol of peace."[8] I agree. A song written by John Calvi says it best: "Some think the army, the bombs and the guns will one day save all of our lives. I don't believe it—heat up your pans. Make peace, and lots of french fries."

Fries will be around for eternity. Scientists from Aristotle University of Thessaloniki in Greece, in conjunction with the European Space Agency, are even attempting to make fries in space,[9] meaning fries will spread beyond globalization into universalization. Average Joes and Joe Martians will enjoy them equally and together. And if fries can help create global peace here on Earth, just think about how important fries will become in the universal peace process after the Alliance to Restore the Republic defeats the Galactic Empire—or did that already happen?

The future of fries is ahead of us.

FRY ON.

The Hippy Chippy fry truck in Peterborough, Ontario.

NOTES

Introduction

1. Brian Wansink and Cynthia Sangerman, "Engineering Comfort Foods," *American Demographics* (July 2000): 66–67.

2. Tom Sietsema, interview by Michel Martin, "Fine Dining Turns to Familiar Favorites," National Public Radio, 6:54, October 24, 2012, http://www.npr.org/2012/10/24/163548909/fine-dining-turns-to-familiar-favorites.

3. Jack F. Loves, *Behind the Arches* (New York: Bantam Dell, 1986), 61.

4. Eric Schlosser, *Fast Food Nation: The Dark Side of the All-American Meal* (New York: Houghton Mifflin, 2001), 115.

5. Karen Hess, "The Origin of French Fries," *Petits propos culinaires* 68 (2001): 39.

6. Wansink and Sangerman, "Engineering Comfort Foods."

7. Stephanie Pappas, "Happiness Linked to Patriotism, Especially in Poor Countries," LiveScience, February 9, 2011, http://www.livescience.com/12791-happiness-linked-patriotism.html.

8. Kathleen DesMaisons, *Potatoes Not Prozac* (New York: Simon & Schuster Paperbacks, 2008), 143.

9. Eric G. Krause, Annette D. de Kloet, Jonathan N. Flak, Michael D. Smeltzer, Matia B. Solomon, Nathan K. Evanson, Stephen C. Woods, Randall R. Sakai, and James P. Herman, "Hydration State Controls Stress Responsiveness and Social Behavior," *Journal of Neuroscience* 31, no. 14 (April 2011): 5470–76.

Chapter One

1. Charles Q. Choi, "Human Evolution: The Origin of Tool Use," LiveScience, November 11, 2009, http://www.livescience.com/7968-human-evolution-origin-tool.html.

2. Ian Sample, "Cooking May Be 1.9m Years Old, Say Scientists," *Guardian*, August 22, 2011, http://www.theguardian.com/science/2011/aug/22/cooking-origins-homo-erectus.

3. Eddie Wrenn, "Humans Began Eating Plants 180,000 Years Ago," *Daily Mail*, September 21, 2012, http://www.dailymail.co.uk/sciencetech/article-2206544/Humans-began-eating-plants-180-000-years-ago-aid-brain-development---affecting-diet-today.html.

4. I. D. Morton, "Geography and History of the Frying Process," *Grasas y aceites* 49, nos. 3–4 (1998): 247–49.

5. Leviticus 2:7 (New International Version).

6. Numbers 11:5 (New International Version).

7. Reay Tannahill, *Food in History* (New York: Broadway Books, 1995), 53–54.

8. Joseph Dommers Vehling, trans., *Apicius: Cookery and Dining in Imperial Rome* (Mineola, NY: Dover, 1977), 12.

9. Victoria R. Rumble, *Soup Through the Ages* (Jefferson, NC: McFarland, 2009), 25.

10. "Pullam Frontonianum (Chicken a la Fronto)," trans. Micaela Pantke, "Antique Roman Dishes—Collection," July 22, 1993, Carnegie Mellon School of Computer Science Recipe Archive,

http://www.cs.cmu.edu/~mjw/recipes/ethnic/historical/ant-rom-coll.html#10. From Robert Maier, *Das römische Kochbuch des Apicius* (Stuttgart: Reclam, 1992), a translation of Marcus Gavius Apicius, *De re coquinaria* (ca. fourth–fifth century).

11. John Reader, *Potato: A History of the Propitious Esculent* (New Haven, CT: Yale University Press, 2009), 4.

12. Ibid., 50.

13. Ibid., 38.

14. Ibid., 90.

15. "Tempura—or Is It Tapas?" *Sunday Morning Herald*, May 12, 2008, http://www.smh.com.au/news/culture/tempura--or-is-it-tapas/2008/05/12/1210444507708.html.

16. Charles Ebeling, "French Fried: From Monticello to the Moon—A Social, Political, and Cultural Appreciation of the French Fry," *Chicago Literary Club*, October 31, 2005, http://www.chilit.org/docs.ashx?id=174401.

17. Paul Ilegems, *De Frietkotcultuur: het laatste boek over Belgie* (Belgium: Loempia, 1993).

18. Ebeling, "French Fried."

19. See Katie Straw, "Facts You Never Knew About French Fries," The Blog Basket, accessed October 8, 2015, http://www.gourmetgiftbaskets.com/Blog/post/Facts-You-Never-Knew-About-French-Fries.aspx; Frances Robinson, "In Belgium, Potato Fans Fret Over Fate of Frites," *Wall Street Journal*, September 17, 2011, http://www.wsj.com/news/articles/SB10001424053111903927204576573201537015890; "10 Bizarre fact about french fries," Food Revolt, December 4, 2014, http://foodrevolt.com/10-bizarre-fact-french-fries/.

20. Menon, *Les soupers de la cour* (Paris: Guillin, 1755), 150.

21. Pierre Leclercq, "La véritable histoire de la pomme de terre frite," *Culture: le magazine culturel en ligne de l'Université de Liège*, July 12, 2014, http://culture.ulg.ac.be/jcms/c_13056/fr/la-veritable-histoire-de-la-pomme-de-terre-frite-1re-partie.

22. Coolidge Collection of Thomas Jefferson Manuscripts 1705–1827, Massachusetts Historical Society, Boston; see Karen Hess, "The Origin of French Fries," *Petits propos culinaires* 68 (2001): 40.

23. Ibid., 43.

24. Ebeling, "French Fried."

Chapter Two

1. "Our Products," McCain Foods, accessed June 1, 2014, http://www.mccain.com/GoodFood/Pages/products.aspx.

2. "Frozen Fries," *How It's Made*, Discovery Science Channel (Silver Spring, MD: October 6, 2010).

3. "A Fresh Look at Frozen Potatoes," Lamb Weston, accessed December 5, 2014, http://www.lambweston.com/assets/resources/Fresh_Vs_Frozen.pdf.

4. Eric Schlosser, *Fast Food Nation: The Dark Side of the All-American Meal* (New York: Houghton Mifflin, 2001), 117.

5. Andrew F. Smith, *Potato: A Global History* (London: Reaktion, 2011), 76.

6. Schlosser, *Fast Food Nation*, 118.

7. Brad Plumer, "After a 70-Year Drop, Small Farms Make a (Small) Comeback," *Washington Post*, October 2, 2012, http://www.washingtonpost.com/blogs/wonkblog/wp/2012/10/02/after-a-70-year-drop-farming-makes-a-small-comeback/.

8. Stephen Daniells, "US Organic Food Market to Grow 14% from 2013–18," Food Navigator USA, January 3, 2014, http://www.foodnavigator-usa.com/Markets/US-organic-food-market-to-grow-14-from-2013-18.

9. "2012 Census of Agriculture," US Department of Agriculture, May 2014, http://www.agcensus.usda.gov/Publications/2012/Full_Report/Volume_1,_Chapter_1_US/usv1.pdf.

10. Michael Blaustein, "Belgium Gets Rolls Royce of Vending Machines—Fresh French Fries in 90 Seconds Flat," *New York Post*, August 19, 2013, http://nypost.com/2013/08/19/belgium-gets-rolls-royce-of-vending-machines-fresh-french-fries-in-90-seconds-flat/.

11. Pierre Leclercq, "La véritable histoire de la pomme de terre frite," *Culture: le magazine culturel en ligne de l'Université de Liège*, July 12, 2014, http://culture.ulg.ac.be/jcms/c_13056/fr/la-veritable-histoire-de-la-pomme-de-terre-frite-1re-partie.

12. Potato Chip Museum, *The History of Fried Potatoes* (Bruges, Belgium: Frietmuseum, 2013), 29.

13. "La frite est-elle Belge ou Française?" *Le point*, December 28, 2012, http://www.lepoint.fr/insolite/la-frite-est-elle-belge-ou-francaise-28-12-2012-1606534_48.php.

Chapter Three

1. "Potatoes," US Department of Agriculture, Economic Research Service, October 7, 2014, http://www.ers.usda.gov/topics/crops/vegetables-pulses/potatoes.aspx.

2. John Reader, *Potato: A History of the Propitious Esculent* (New Haven, CT: Yale University Press, 2009), 4.

3. Ibid., 5.

4. Michael Pollan, *The Botany of Desire* (New York: Random House, 2002), Kindle edition, chap. 4.

5. American Chemical Society, "Largest USDA Study of Food Antioxidants Reveals Best Sources," *ScienceDaily*, accessed July 16, 2015, www.sciencedaily.com/releases/2004/06/040617080908.htm.

6. Jennie Brand-Miller, Kaye Foster-Powell, and Philippa Sandall, *The New Glucose Revolution: Low GI Eating Made Easy* (New York: Marlowe, 2005), Kindle edition, part 4.

7. Christiane Northrup, "Now Saturated Fat Is Good for You?" *Huffington Post*, March 26, 2014, http://www.huffingtonpost.com/christiane-northrup/saturated-fat_b_4914235.html.

8. Nicoletta Pellegrini, Cristiana Miglio, Daniele Del Rio, Sara Salvatore, Mauro Serafini, and Furio Brighenti, "Effect of Domestic Cooking Methods on the Total Antioxidant Capacity of Vegetables," *International Journal of Food Sciences*

and Nutrition 60 (2009): 12–22.

9. "When Popular Meets Profitable, That's the Sweet Spot," McCain Foods, 2013, http://www.mccainusafoodservice.com/uploads/media/original/brc646_lr.pdf.

10. "Sweet Things," Lamb Weston, accessed October 8, 2015, http://www.notjustanotherfry.com.

11. L.G.M. Baas-Becking, "Historical Notes on Salt and Salt-Manufacturing," *Scientific Monthly* 32, no. 5 (May 1931): 434–46.

12. "History of Salt," Saltworks, accessed December 5, 2014, http://www.saltworks.us/salt_info/si_HistoryOfSalt.asp.

13. Mark Kurlansky, *Salt: A World History* (New York: Walker, 2002), 8.

14. Ibid., 5.

15. Eric G. Krause, Annette D. de Kloet, Jonathan N. Flak, Michael D. Smeltzer, Matia B. Solomon, Nathan K. Evanson, Stephen C. Woods, Randall R. Sakai, and James P. Herman, "Hydration State Controls Stress Responsiveness and Social Behavior," *Journal of Neuroscience* 31, no. 14 (April 2011): 5470–76.

16. Andrew F. Smith, *Pure Ketchup* (Columbia: University of South Carolina Press, 1996), 21.

17. Ibid., 125.

18. Roberto A. Ferdman and Ritchie King, "Ketchup Isn't the King of American Condiments. Mayonnaise Is," *Quartz*, January 30, 2014, http://qz.com/172019/ketchup-isnt-the-king-of-american-condiments-mayonnaise-is/.

19. Brock Vergakis, "My Oh My Do We Love Fry Sauce!" *Deseret News*, January 6, 2007, http://www.deseretnews.com/article/650220850/My-oh-my-do-we-love-fry-sauce.html?pg=all.

20. Charles Q. Choi, "Beer Lubricated the Rise of Civilization, Study Suggests," LiveScience, November 5, 2010, http://www.livescience.com/10221-beer-lubricated-rise-civilization-study-suggests.html.

21. Max Nelson, *The Barbarian's Beverage: A History of Beer in Ancient Europe* (New York: Routledge, 2005), 1.

Chapter Four

1. "Chip Pans," *Cambridgeshire Fire and Rescue Service*, accessed December 5, 2014, http://www.cambsfire.gov.uk/firesafety/94.php.

2. Charles Ebeling, "French Fried: From Monticello to the Moon: A Social, Political, and Cultural Appreciation of the French Fry," *Chicago Literary Club*, October 31, 2005, http://www.chilit.org/docs.ashx?id=174401.

Chapter Five

1. "Commodities by Country," FAOStat, accessed December 5, 2014, http://faostat.fao.org/site/339/default.aspx.

2. John Reader, *Potato: A History of the Propitious Esculent* (New Haven, CT: Yale University Press, 2009), 267.

3. "Belge ou française? Le mystère des origines de la frite persiste," *Le Parisien*, December 28, 2012, http://www.leparisien.fr/flash-actualite-culture/belge-ou-

francaise-le-mystere-des-origines-de-la-frite-persiste-28-12-2012-2439605.php.

4. John Helliwell, Richard Layard, and Jeffrey Sachs, "World Happiness Report 2013," United Nations Sustainable Development Solutions Network, 2013, http://unsdsn.org/wp-content/uploads/2014/02/WorldHappinessReport2013_online.pdf.

5. "The Global 30," *QSR*, 2011, http://www.qsrmagazine.com/content/global-30.

6. Patra Wroten, "Americans Don't Want to Share Their Fries with the President," FedScoop, July 11, 2014, http://fedscoop.com/americans-dont-want-share-fries-president/.

7. Helliwell, Layard, and Sachs, "World Happiness Report 2013."

8. Kate Sekulles, "A Staple from Quebec, Embarrassing but Adored," *New York Times*, May 23, 2007, http://www.nytimes.com/2007/05/23/dining/23pout.html?_r=2&.

9. Katie Straw, "Facts You Never Knew About French Fries," The Blog Basket, accessed October 8, 2015, http://www.gourmetgiftbaskets.com/Blog/post/Facts-You-Never-Knew-About-French-Fries.aspx.

10. Michael Martinez, "Is Kim Jong Un Still in Charge of North Korea?" CNN World, October 8, 2014, http://www.cnn.com/2014/10/07/world/asia/north-korea-where-is-kim-jong-un/.

11. Amanda Mannen, "6 Famous Documentaries That Were Shockingly Full of Crap," *Cracked*, August 12, 2013, http://www.cracked.com/article_20585_6-famous-documentaries-that-were-shockingly-full-crap.html#ixzz3KfeILxOO.

12. Leigh Richards, "What Industry Spends the Most on Advertising," *Houston Chronicle*, accessed December 5, 2014, http://smallbusiness.chron.com/industry-spends-advertising-22512.html.

13. "Infographic: Meet America's 25 Biggest Advertisers," *Advertising Age*, July 8, 2013, http://adage.com/article/news/meet-america-s-25-biggest-advertisers/242969/.

14. Chris O'Brien, "Twitter Explains Why 'Soggy Fries' May Be Key to Its Big Data Future," VentureBeat, November 5, 2014, http://venturebeat.com/2014/11/05/twitter-revenue-chief-explains-why-soggy-fries-may-be-key-to-its-big-data-future/.

15. Kristin Jarratt, "Ostia Antica: The Better Pompeii," *In Italy*, http://www.initaly.com/regions/latium/ostia.htm.

Epilogue

1. Peter Pham, "10 Mind-Blowing Food Trends Already Dominating 2014," Foodbeast, April 24, 2014, http://www.foodbeast.com/2014/04/24/food-trends-2014/.

2. Ben Sobel, "Move Over, Ramen Burger: The French Fry–Stuffed Burrito Is California's Secret Frankenfood," *GQ*, September, 25, 2013, http://www.gq.com/blogs/the-q/2013/09/move-over-ramen-burger-the-french-fry-stuffed-burrito-is-californias-secret-frankenfood.html.

3. Jason Mick, "Wendy's New 'Natural' Fries Caught Using Chemical Stew," Daily Tech, April 16, 2011, http://www.dailytech.com/Natural+Fries+Caught+Using+Chemical+Stew/article21394.htm.

4. Zack Kyle, "McDonald's Rejects Simplot's Genetically Modified Potato," *Idaho Statesman*, November 15, 2014, http://www.idahostatesman.com/2014/11/15/3487642_mcdonalds-rejects-simplots-gmo.html?rh=1.

5. "Great News from Mediterranean Diet Experts: French Fries Are Good for You!," Worldcrunch/*La stampa*, November 30, 2012, http://www.worldcrunch.com/food-travel/great-news-from-mediterranean-diet-experts-french-fries-are-good-for-you-/healthy-frying-french-fries-naples-oil/c6s10281/#.VH8STItWJ8b.

6. "Who Eats the Most Fast Food?" Market Research World, accessed December 5, 2014, http://www.marketresearchworld.net/content/view/1082/77.

7. "Renewable Fuel Standard Program (RFS2) Regulatory Impact Analysis," Assessment and Standards Division, Office of Transportation and Air Quality, US Environmental Protection Agency, February 2010, http://www.epa.gov/otaq/renewablefuels/420r10006.pdf.

8. Natalia Sloam, "10 Things You Didn't Know About French Fries," *Daily Meal*, July 11, 2014, http://www.thedailymeal.com/10-things-you-didn-t-know-about-french-fries.

9. Philip Ball, "Astronaut Food: Can You Cook Fries in Space?" BBC, December 19, 2013, http://www.bbc.com/future/story/20131219-can-astronauts-cook-fries.

CREDITS

ACKNOWLEDGMENTS

Andrea, thank you. You have loved and supported me throughout our marriage—even when I told you I wanted to leave a promising government career to make fries. I love you. And I'm stoked to love you through this life and the next.

Riley, thank you. You put your faith in BFC and me. You taught me how to run a restaurant. You've been an incredible business partner. I look forward to growing our businesses together.

BFC fry associates, thank you. Owners get entirely too much credit for running businesses. Your diligence has made BFC the success it is today. I'm grateful and blessed to work alongside you.

PUBLISHED BY

Princeton Architectural Press
37 East Seventh Street
New York, New York 10003

Visit our website at www.papress.com.

EDITOR: Sara Stemen
DESIGNER: Mia Johnson

SPECIAL THANKS TO: Nicola Bednarek Brower, Janet Behning, Erin Cain, Tom Cho,
Barbara Darko, Benjamin English, Jenny Florence, Jan Cigliano Hartman, Jan Haux,
Lia Hunt, Valerie Kamen, Simone Kaplan-Senchak, Stephanie Leke, Diane Levinson,
Jennifer Lippert, Sara McKay, Jaime Nelson Noven, Rob Shaeffer, Paul Wagner,
Joseph Weston, and Janet Wong of Princeton Architectural Press
—Kevin C. Lippert, publisher

Library of Congress Cataloging-in-Publication Data
Lingle, Blake.
Fries! : an illustrated guide to the world's favorite food / Blake Lingle. — First edition.
    pages   cm
Includes bibliographical references.
ISBN 978-1-61689-458-0 (alk. paper)
1. French fries. I. Title.
TX803.P8L56 2016
641.6'521—dc23
                    2015021323